C000185693

SCRIPTURES
FOR
PRAYER

by
Stephen & Barbara Arbo

He sends forth His Word and heals them and rescues,
them from the pit and destruction.
Psalm 107:20

Copyright 1980, revised 2003, 2023 by Stephen and Barbara Arbo
ISBN: 979-8-9874866-4-1

All Rights Reserved

Printed in the United States of America

Unless otherwise indicated, all Scripture quotations are taken from the Amplified Bible, Classic Edition as shown below.

Scripture quotations taken from the Amplified® Bible Classic, Copyright © 1954, 1958, 1962, 1964, 1965, 1987 by The Lockman Foundation. Used by permission. (www.Lockman.org)

Scripture quotations marked (BSB) are taken from The Holy Bible, Berean Study Bible, BSB. Copyright ©2016, 2018 by Bible Hub. Used by Permission. All Rights Reserved Worldwide. www.berean.bible

Scripture quotations marked (NIV) are taken from the Holy Bible, New International Version®, NIV®. Copyright © 1973, 1978, 1984 by Biblica, Inc.™ Used by permission of Zondervan. All rights reserved worldwide.

Scripture quotations marked (KJV) are taken from the Holy Bible, King James Version (Public Domain).

Text Design: Lisa Simpson
SimpsonProductions.net

DEDICATION

Much heartfelt thanks to Billie Adams who shared
her life and ministry of praying God's Word with me,
that I in turn might share it with others.

ACKNOWLEDGEMENT

"For a dream comes with much
business and painful effort."
Ecclesiastes 5:3

1980

None of our dreams can become reality without the hard work of those willing to invest their gifts to help fulfill those dreams. Thank you once again, Barbara Pendleton, for juggling your time and energy as a new mother to get this book in print.

I pray Janie will always have "great peace and undisturbed composure." (Isaiah 54:13)

2023

Through the years, God has brought so many gifts into my life in the form of tech-savvy people and creative designers, all of whom have not only been a blessing to the ministry but are also dear friends.

My heart is so grateful for Renae Cockroft's expertise and joyfully investing in this project to see our vision for legacy fulfilled and to Christa Baca for her creative design of the cover.

I want to acknowledge each of you as readers, who have used this book for the past decades, covered it with tears and coffee stains, and have seen God watch over His word to perform it. I celebrate each answer to prayer with you! Order a fresh book, gift it to friends, spread it through prayer groups, and let's leave a legacy of praying God's word to the next generation.

Renae Cockroft
Virtual Assistant
Rc4jesus@gmail.com

Christa Baca
Graphic Design
cbaca@gointernational.tv

Lisa Simpson
Text Design
SimpsonProductions.net

Foreword

The original version of *'Scriptures for Prayer'* was printed in 1980 for each of you whose requests for a copy of our prayer notebook inspired us to share it. Much has happened in our world in 40-plus years, and we have grown to appreciate, more than ever, the confidence in praying God's will through His Word. Our nations, national leaders, our own churches and families need our prayers like never before.

In no way does this notebook cover all the scriptures on any given subject; and, many are not directly quoted scriptures, but rather the scripture's context in prayer or topical form. Praying God's Word is not meant to be a ritual, but rather to acquaint ourselves with God's known will, that we might know His heart and follow His directives in prayer.

As we have sent forth God's Word in prayer, it has not returned void in our lives, and so shall it be in your lives, for God is faithful to His Word, and will hasten to watch over His Word to perform it! (Isaiah 5:11, Jeremiah 1:12).

If you live in Me abide vitally united to Me and My words remain in you and continue to live in your hearts, ask whatever you will, and it shall be done for you...I have told you these things that your joy may be full… (John 15:7,11)

We trust you will continue to grow with us in prayer with this expanded edition of 'Scriptures for Prayer.'

In His Love,
Stephen & Barbara Arbo

NOTE: Where there is an underline (_____)
just fill in the people or places that you are
praying about to personalize your prayer.

TABLE OF CONTENTS

1

For Our President, Leaders, and Those in Authority

Exodus 15:2 & 22

> The Lord is my Strength and my Song, and He has become my Salvation; this is my God, and I will praise Him, my father's God, and I will exalt Him.

2 Chronicles 1:10

> Give me now wisdom and knowledge to go out and come in before this people, for who can rule this Your people who are so great?

Psalm 18:1-6

> I love You fervently and devotedly, O Lord, my Strength. The Lord is my Rock, my fortress, and my Deliverer; my God, my keen and firm Strength in Whom I will trust and take refuge, my shield, and the Horn of my salvation, my High Tower. I will call upon the Lord, who is to be praised; so shall I be saved from my enemies. The cords or bands of death surrounded me, and the streams

of ungodliness and the torrents of ruin terrified me. The cords of Sheol (the place of the dead) surrounded me; the snares of death confronted and came upon me. In my distress when seemingly closed in I called upon the Lord and cried to my God; He heard my voice out of His temple (heavenly dwelling place), and my cry came before Him, into His very ears.

Psalm 119:66, 169

Teach me good judgment, wise and right discernment, and knowledge, for I have believed (trusted, relied on, and clung to) Your commandments. Let my mournful cry and supplication come [near] before You, O Lord; give me understanding (discernment and comprehension) according to Your word [of assurance and promise].

Proverbs 2:1-15

My son, if you will receive my words and treasure up my commandments within you, making your ear attentive to skillful and godly wisdom and inclining and directing your heart and mind to understanding [applying all your powers to the quest for it]; Yes, if you cry out for insight and raise your voice for understanding, If you seek wisdom as for silver and search for skillful and godly wisdom as for hidden treasures, Then you will understand the reverent and worshipful fear of the Lord and find the knowledge of our omniscient God. For the Lord gives skillful and godly Wisdom; from His mouth comes knowledge and understanding. He hides away sound and godly Wisdom and stores it for the righteous (those who are upright and in right standing with Him); He is a shield to those who walk uprightly and in integrity, That He may guard the paths of justice; yes, He preserves the way of His saints. Then you will understand righteousness, justice, and fair dealing [in every area and relation]; yes, you will understand every good path. For skillful and godly wisdom shall enter into your heart, and knowledge shall be pleasant to you. Discretion shall watch over you, understanding shall keep you, to deliver you from the way of evil and the evil men, from men who speak perverse things and are liars, Men who forsake the paths of uprightness to walk in the ways of darkness, Who rejoice to do evil and delight in the perverseness of evil, Who are crooked in their ways, wayward and devious in their paths.

Proverbs 2:20-22

So may you walk in the way of good men and keep to the paths of the consistently righteous (the upright, in right standing with God). For the upright shall dwell in the land, and the men of integrity, blameless and complete in God's sight, shall remain in it; But the wicked shall be cut off from the earth, and the treacherous shall be rooted out of it.

Proverbs 4:11

I have taught you in the way of skillful and godly Wisdom [which is comprehensive insight into the ways and purposes of God]; I have led you in paths of uprightness.

Proverbs 11:3-7

The integrity of the upright shall guide them, but the willful contrariness and crookedness of the treacherous shall destroy them. Riches provide no security in any day of wrath and judgment, but righteousness (uprightness and right standing with God) delivers from death. The righteousness of the blameless shall rectify and make plain their way and keep it straight, but the wicked shall fall by their own wickedness. The righteousness of the upright [their rectitude in every area and relation] shall deliver them, but the treacherous shall be taken in their own iniquity and greedy desire. When the wicked man dies, his hope [for the future] perishes; and the expectation of the godless comes to nothing.

Proverbs 16:10

Divinely directed decisions are on the lips of the king; his mouth should not transgress in judgment.

Proverbs 19:21

Many plans are in a man's mind, but it is the Lord's purpose for him that will stand.

Proverbs 20:26

A wise king winnows out the wicked [from among the good] and brings the threshing wheel over them [to separate the chaff from the grain].

Proverbs 20:28

Loving-kindness and mercy, truth and faithfulness, preserve the king, and his throne is upheld by [the people's] loyalty.

Proverbs 21:1

The king's heart is in the hand of the Lord, as are the watercourses; He turns it whichever way He wills.

Proverbs 21:2

Every way of a man is right in his own eyes, but the Lord weighs and tries the hearts.

Proverbs 28:2

When a land transgresses, it has many rulers, but when the ruler is a man of discernment, understanding, and knowledge, its stability will long continue.

Proverbs 29:2

When the [uncompromisingly] righteous are in authority, the people rejoice; but when the wicked man rules, the people groan and sigh.

Proverbs 29:14

The king who faithfully judges the poor, his throne shall be established continuously.

Isaiah 11:2-5

And the Spirit of the Lord shall rest upon Him -the Spirit of wisdom and understanding, the Spirit of counsel and might, the Spirit of knowledge and of the reverential and obedient fear of the Lord - and shall make Him of quick understanding, and His delight shall be in the reverential and obedient fear of the Lord. And He shall not judge by the sight of His eyes, neither decide by the hearing of His ears; But with righteousness and justice shall He judge the poor and decide with fairness for the meek, the poor, and the downtrodden of the earth; and He shall smite the earth and the oppressor with the rod of His mouth, and with the breath of His lips He shall slay the wicked.

And righteousness shall be the girdle of His waist and faithfulness the girdle of His loins.

Isaiah 40:31

But those who wait for the Lord [who expect, look for, and hope in Him] shall change and renew their strength and power; they shall lift their wings and mount up [close to God] as eagles [mount up to the sun]; they shall run and not be weary, they shall walk and not faint or become tired.

Isaiah 50:4

[The Servant of God says] The Lord God has given Me the tongue of a disciple and of one who is taught, that I should know how to speak a word in season to him who is weary. He wakens Me morning by morning; He wakens My ear to hear as a disciple [as one who is taught].

1 Corinthians 16:13

Be alert and on your guard; stand firm in your faith (your conviction respecting man's relationship to God and divine things, keeping the trust and holy fervor born of faith and a part of it). Act like men and be courageous; grow in strength!

Ephesians 1:17-18

I always pray that the God of our Lord Jesus Christ, the Father of glory, may grant you a spirit of wisdom and of revelation [that gives you a deep and personal and intimate insight] into the true knowledge of Him [for we know the Father through the Son]. And I pray that the eyes of your heart [the very center and core of your being] may be enlightened [flooded with light by the Holy Spirit], so that you will know and cherish the hope [the divine guarantee, the confident expectation] to which He has called you, the riches of His glorious inheritance in the saints (God's people).

James 1:5

If any of you is deficient in wisdom, let him ask of the giving God [Who gives] to everyone liberally and ungrudgingly, without reproaching or faultfinding, and it will be given him.

Leaders

2

FOR THOSE IN THE MILITARY

Deuteronomy 20:1-4

When you go forth to battle against your enemies and see horses and chariots and an army greater than your own, do not be afraid of them, for the Lord your God, Who brought you out of the land of Egypt, is with you. And when you come near to the battle, the priest shall approach and speak to the men, and shall say to them, Hear, O Israel, you draw near this day to battle against your enemies. Let not your [minds and] hearts faint; fear not, and do not tremble or be terrified [and in dread] because of them. For the Lord your God is He Who goes with you to fight for you against your enemies to save you.

2 Samuel 22:33-35

God is my strong Fortress; He guides the blameless in His way and sets him free. He makes my feet like the hinds' [firm and able]; He sets me secure and confident upon the heights. He trains my hands for war, so that my arms can bend a bow of bronze.

2 Samuel 22:38

I have pursued my enemies and destroyed them; and I did not turn back until they were consumed.

2 Kings 19:35

And it all came to pass, for that night the Angel of the Lord went forth and slew 185,000 in the camp of the Assyrians; and when [the living] arose early in the morning, behold, all these were dead bodies.

2 Chronicles 20:12-15

O our God, will You not exercise judgment upon them? For we have no might to stand against this great company that is coming against us. We do not know what to do, but our eyes are upon You. And all Judah stood before the Lord, with their children and their wives. Then the Spirit of the Lord came upon Jahaziel son of Zechariah, the son of Benaiah, the son of Jeiel, the son of Mattaniah, a Levite of the sons of Asaph, in the midst of the assembly. He said, Hearken, all Judah, you inhabitants of Jerusalem, and you King Jehoshaphat. The Lord says this to you: Be not afraid or dismayed at this great multitude; for the battle is not yours, but God's.

2 Chronicles 20:22

And when they began to sing and to praise, the Lord set ambushments against the men of Ammon, Moab, and Mount Seir who had come against Judah, and they were [self-] slaughtered.

Psalm 3

Lord, how they are increased who trouble me! Many are they who rise up against me. Many are saying of me, There is no help for him in God. Selah [pause, and calmly think of that]! But You, O Lord, are a shield for me, my glory, and the lifter of my head. With my voice I cry to the Lord, and He hears and answers me out of His holy hill. Selah [pause, and calmly think of that]! I lay down and slept; I wakened again, for the Lord sustains me. I will not be afraid of ten thousands of people who have set themselves against me round about. Arise, O Lord; save me, O my God! For You have struck all my enemies on the cheek; You have broken the teeth of the ungodly. Salvation belongs to the Lord; May Your blessing be upon Your people. Selah [pause, and calmly think of that]!

Psalm 18:1-3

I love You fervently and devotedly, O Lord, my Strength. The Lord is my Rock, my Fortress, and my Deliverer; my God, my keen and firm Strength in Whom I will trust and take refuge, my Shield, and the Horn of my salvation, my High Tower. I will call upon the Lord, who is to be praised; so shall I be saved from my enemies.

Psalm 27:1-14

The Lord is my Light and my Salvation—whom shall I fear or dread? The Lord is the Refuge and Stronghold of my life—of whom shall I be afraid? When the wicked, even my enemies and my foes, came upon me to eat up my flesh, they stumbled and fell. Though a host encamp against me, my heart shall not fear; though war arise against me, [even then] in this will I be confident. One thing have I asked of the Lord, that will I seek, inquire for, and [insistently] require: that I may dwell in the house of the Lord [in His presence] all the days of my life, to behold and gaze upon the beauty [the sweet attractiveness and the delightful loveliness] of the Lord and to meditate, consider, and inquire in His temple. For in the day of trouble He will hide me in His shelter; in the secret place of His tent will He hide me; He will set me high upon a rock. And now shall my head be lifted up above my enemies round about me; in His tent I will offer sacrifices and shouting of joy; I will sing, yes, I will sing praises to the Lord. Hear, O Lord, when I cry aloud; have mercy and be gracious to me and answer me! You have said, Seek My face [inquire for and require My presence as your vital need]. My heart says to You, Your face (Your presence), Lord, will I seek, inquire for, and require [of necessity and on the authority of Your Word]. Hide not Your face from me; turn not Your servant away in anger, You Who have been my help! Cast me not off, neither forsake me, O God of my salvation! Although my father and my mother have forsaken me, yet the Lord will take me up [adopt me as His child]. Teach me Your way, O Lord, and lead me in a plain and even path because of my enemies [those who lie in wait for me]. Give me not up to the will of my adversaries, for false witnesses have risen up against me; they breathe out cruelty and violence. What, what would have become of me had I not believed that I would see the Lord's goodness in the land of the living! Wait and hope for and expect the Lord; be brave and of good courage and let your heart be stout and enduring. Yes, wait for and hope for and expect the Lord.

Psalm 34:21-22

Evil shall cause the death of the wicked; and they who hate the just and righteous shall be held guilty and shall be condemned. The Lord redeems the lives of His servants, and none of those who take refuge and trust in Him shall be condemned or held guilty.

Psalm 35:1-10

Contend, O Lord, with those who contend with me; fight against those who fight against me! Take hold of shield and buckler and stand up for my help! Draw out also the spear and javelin and close up the way of those who pursue and persecute me. Say to me, I am your deliverance! Let them be put to shame and dishonor who seek and require my life; let them be turned back and confounded who plan my hurt! Let them be as chaff before the wind, with the Angel of the Lord driving them on! Let their way be through dark and slippery places, with the Angel of the Lord pursuing and afflicting them. For without cause they hid for me their net; a pit of destruction without cause they dug for my life. Let destruction befall my foe unawares; let the net he hid for me catch him; let him fall into that very destruction. Then I shall be joyful in the Lord; I shall rejoice in His deliverance. All my bones shall say, Lord, who is like You, You Who deliver the poor and the afflicted from him who is too strong for him, yes, the poor and the needy from him who snatches away his goods?

Military

Psalm 37:1-40

Fret not yourself because of evildoers, neither be envious against those who work unrighteousness (that which is not upright or in right standing with God). For they shall soon be cut down like the grass, and wither as the green herb. Trust (lean on, rely on, and be confident) in the Lord and do good; so, shall you dwell in the land and feed surely on His faithfulness, and truly you shall be fed. Delight yourself also in the Lord, and He will give you the desires and secret petitions of your heart. Commit your way to the Lord [roll and repose each care of your load on Him]; trust (lean on, rely on, and be confident) also in Him and He will bring it to pass. And He will make your uprightness and right standing with God go forth as the light, and your justice and right as [the shining sun of] the noonday. Be still and rest in the Lord; wait for Him and patiently lean yourself upon Him; fret not yourself because of him who prospers in his way, because of the man who brings wicked devices to pass. Cease from anger and forsake wrath; fret not yourself - it tends only to evildoing. For evildoers shall be cut off, but those who wait and hope and look for the Lord [in the end] shall inherit the earth. For yet a little while, and the evildoers will be no more; though you look with care where they used to be, they will not be found. But the meek [in the end] shall inherit the earth and shall delight themselves in the abundance of peace. The wicked plot against the [uncompromisingly] righteous (the upright in right standing with God); they gnash at them with their teeth. The Lord laughs at [the wicked], for He sees that their own day [of defeat] is coming. The wicked draw the sword and bend their bows to cast down the poor and needy, to slay those who walk uprightly (blameless in conduct and in conversation). The swords [of the wicked] shall enter their own hearts, and their bows shall be broken. Better is the little that the uncompromisingly righteous have than the abundance [of possessions] of many who are wrong and wicked. For the arms of the wicked shall be broken, but the Lord upholds the [consistently] righteous. The Lord knows the days of the upright and blameless, and their heritage will abide forever. They shall not be put to shame in the time of evil; and in the days of famine, they shall be satisfied. But the wicked shall perish, and the enemies of the Lord shall be as the fat of lambs [that is consumed in smoke] and as the glory of the pastures. They shall vanish; like smoke shall they consume away. The wicked borrow and pay not again [for they may be unable], but the [uncompromisingly] righteous deal kindly and give [for they are able]. For such as are blessed of God shall [in the end] inherit the earth, but they that are cursed of Him shall be cut off. The steps of a [good] man are directed and established by the Lord when He delights in his way [and He busies Himself with his every step]. Though he falls, he shall not be utterly cast down, for the Lord grasps his hand in support and upholds him. I have been young and now am old, yet have I not seen the [uncompromisingly] righteous forsaken or their seed begging bread. All day long they are merciful and deal graciously; they lend, and their offspring are blessed. Depart from evil and do good; and you will dwell forever [securely]. For the Lord delights in justice and forsakes not His saints; they are preserved

Military

forever, but the offspring of the wicked [in time] shall be cut off. Then the [consistently] righteous shall inherit the land and dwell upon it forever. The mouth of the [uncompromisingly] righteous utters wisdom, and his tongue speaks with justice. The law of his God is in his heart; none of his steps shall slide. The wicked lie in wait for the [uncompromisingly] righteous and seek to put them to death. The Lord will not leave them in their hands, or [suffer them to] condemn them when they are judged. Wait for and expect the Lord and keep and heed His way, and He will exalt you to inherit the land; [in the end] when the wicked are cut off, you shall see it. I have seen a wicked man in great power and spreading himself like a green tree in its native soil, yet he passed away, and behold, he was not; yes, I sought and inquired for him, but he could not be found. Mark the blameless man and behold the upright, for there is a happy end for the man of peace. As for transgressors, they shall be destroyed together; in the end the wicked shall be cut off. But the salvation of the [consistently] righteous is of the Lord; He is their Refuge and secure Stronghold in the time of trouble. And the Lord helps them and delivers them; He delivers them from the wicked and saves them, because they trust and take refuge in Him.

Psalm 91:1-16

He who dwells in the secret place of the Most High shall remain stable and fixed under the shadow of the Almighty [Whose power no foe can withstand]. I will say of the Lord, He is my Refuge and my Fortress, my God; on Him I lean and rely, and in Him I [confidently] trust!

For [then] He will deliver you from the snare of the fowler and from the deadly pestilence. [Then] He will cover you with His pinions, and under His wings shall you trust and find refuge; His truth and His faithfulness are a shield and a buckler. You shall not be afraid of the terror of the night, nor of the arrow (the evil plots and slanders of the wicked) that flies by day, Nor of the pestilence that stalks in darkness, nor of the destruction and sudden death that surprise and lay waste at noonday. A thousand may fall at your side, and ten thousand at your right hand, but it shall not come near you. Only a spectator shall you be [yourself inaccessible in the secret place of the Most High] as you witness the reward of the wicked. Because you have made the Lord your refuge, and the Most High your dwelling place, there shall no evil befall you, nor any plague or calamity come near your tent. For He will give His angels [especial] charge over you to accompany and defend and preserve you in all your ways [of obedience and service]. They shall bear you up on their hands, lest you dash your foot against a stone. You shall tread upon the lion and adder; the young lion and the serpent shall you trample underfoot. Because he has set his love upon Me, therefore will I deliver him; I will set him on high, because he knows and understands My name [has a personal knowledge of My mercy, love, and kindness - trusts and relies on Me, knowing I will never forsake him, no, never]. He shall call upon Me, and I will answer him; I will be with him in trouble, I will deliver him and honor him. With long life will I satisfy him and show him My salvation.

Psalm 112:7

He shall not be afraid of evil tidings; his heart is firmly fixed, trusting (leaning on and being confident) in the Lord.

Isaiah 31:3

Now the Egyptians are men and not God, and their horses are flesh and not spirit; and when the Lord stretches out His hand, both [Egypt] who helps will stumble, and [Judah] who is helped will fall, and they will all perish and be consumed together.

Isaiah 40:29

He gives power to the faint and weary, and to him who has no might He increases strength [causing it to multiply and making it to abound].

Isaiah 41:10-13

Fear not [there is nothing to fear], for I am with you; do not look around you in terror and be dismayed, for I am your God. I will strengthen and harden you to difficulties, yes, I will help you; yes, I will hold you up and retain you with My [victorious] right hand of rightness and justice. Behold, all they who are enraged and inflamed against you shall be put to shame and confounded; they who strive against you shall be as nothing and shall perish. You shall seek those who contend with you but shall not find them; they who war against you shall be as nothing, as nothing at all. For I the Lord your God hold your right hand; I am the Lord, Who says to you, Fear not; I will help you!

Isaiah 54:14

You shall establish yourself in righteousness (rightness, in conformity with God's will and order): you shall be far from even the thought of oppression or destruction, for you shall not fear, and from terror, for it shall not come near you.

Isaiah 54:17

But no weapon that is formed against you shall prosper, and every tongue that shall rise against you in judgment you shall show to be in the wrong. This [peace, righteousness, security, triumph over opposition] is the heritage of the servants of the Lord [those in whom the ideal Servant of the Lord is reproduced]; this is the righteousness or the vindication which they obtain from Me [this is that which I impart to them as their justification], says the Lord.

2 Corinthians 10:4

For the weapons of our warfare are not physical [weapons of flesh and blood], but they are mighty before God for the overthrow and destruction of strongholds.

Military

3

FOR THE UNVEILING OF HIDDEN THINGS

2 Kings 6:8-13

When the king of Syria was warring against Israel, after counseling with his servants, he said, in such and such a place shall be my camp. Then the man of God sent to the king of Israel, saying, Beware that you pass not such a place, for the Syrians are coming down there. Then the king of Israel sent to the place of which [Elisha] told and warned him; and thus, he protected and saved himself there repeatedly. Therefore, the mind of the king of Syria was greatly troubled by this thing. He called his servants and said, Will you show me who of us is for the king of Israel? One of his servants said, None, my lord O king; but Elisha, the prophet who is in Israel, tells the king of Israel the words that you speak in your bedchamber. He said, Go and see where he is, that I may send and seize him. And it was told him, He is in Dothan.

Job 5:12-13

He frustrates the devices of the crafty, so that their hands cannot perform their enterprise or anything of [lasting] worth. He catches the [so-called] wise in their own trickiness, and the counsel of the schemers is brought to a quick end.

Psalm 55:9

Destroy [their schemes], O Lord, confuse their tongues, for I have seen violence and strife in the city.

Psalm 68:1-3

God is [already] beginning to arise, and His enemies to scatter; let them also who hate Him flee before Him! As smoke is driven away, so drive them away; as wax melts before the fire, so let the wicked perish before the presence of God. But let the [uncompromisingly] righteous be glad; let them be in high spirits and glory before God, yes, let them [jubilantly] rejoice!

Jeremiah 29:11-14

For I know the thoughts and plans that I have for you, says the Lord, thoughts and plans for welfare and peace and not for evil, to give you hope in your final outcome. Then you will call upon Me, and you will come and pray to Me, and I will hear and heed you. Then you will seek Me, inquire for, and require Me [as a vital necessity] and find Me when you search for Me with all your heart. I will be found by you, says the Lord, and I will release you from captivity and gather you from all the nations and all the places to which I have driven you, says the Lord, and I will bring you back to the place from which I caused you to be carried away captive.

Jeremiah 49:10

But I have stripped Esau (Edom) bare; I have uncovered his hiding places, and he cannot hide himself. His offspring will be destroyed, with his brethren and his neighbors; and he will be no more.

Luke 8:17

For there is nothing hidden that shall not be disclosed, nor anything secret that shall not be known and come out into the open.

4

PROTECTION AND GUIDANCE

Deuteronomy 28:6

> Blessed shall you be when you come in and blessed shall you be when you go out.

Psalm 16:1

> Keep and protect me, O God, for in You I have found refuge, and in You do I put my trust and hide myself.

Psalm 18:2

> The Lord is my Rock, my Fortress, and my Deliverer; my God, my keen and firm Strength in Whom I will trust and take refuge, my Shield, and the Horn of my salvation, my High Tower.

Psalm 27:5

> For in the day of trouble He will hide me in His shelter; in the secret place of His tent will He hide me; He will set me high upon a rock.

Psalm 33:10-11

> The Lord brings the counsel of the nations to nought; He makes the thoughts and plans of the peoples of no effect.

The counsel of the Lord stands forever, the thoughts of His heart through all generations.

Psalm 34:17

When the righteous cry for help, the Lord hears, and delivers them out of all their distress and troubles.

Psalm 34:19-20

Many evils confront the [consistently] righteous, but the Lord delivers him out of them all. He keeps all his bones; not one of them is broken.

Psalm 35:1

Contend, O Lord, with those who contend with me; fight against those who fight against me!

Psalm 37:23

The steps of a [good] man are directed and established by the Lord when he delights in his way [and he busies himself with his every step].

Psalm 57:1-2

Be merciful and gracious to me, O God, be merciful and gracious to me, for my soul takes refuge and finds shelter and confidence in You; yes, in the shadow of Your wings will I take refuge and be confident until calamities and destructive storms are passed. I will cry to God Most High, Who performs on my behalf and rewards me [Who brings to pass His purposes for me and surely completes them]!

Psalm 91

He who dwells in the secret place of the Most High shall remain stable and fixed under the shadow of the Almighty [Whose power no foe can withstand]. I will say of the Lord, He is my Refuge and my Fortress, my God; on Him I lean and rely, and in Him I [confidently] trust! For [then] He will deliver you from the snare of the fowler and from the deadly pestilence. [Then] He will cover you with His pinions, and under His wings shall you trust and find refuge; His truth and His faithfulness are a shield and a buckler. You shall not be afraid of the terror of the night, nor of the arrow (the evil plots and slanders of the wicked) that flies by day, Nor of the pestilence that stalks in darkness, nor of the destruction and sudden death that surprise and lay waste at noonday. A thousand may fall at your side, and ten thousand at your right hand, but it shall not come near you. Only a spectator shall you be [yourself inaccessible in the secret place of the Most High] as you witness the reward of the wicked. Because you have made the Lord your refuge, and the Most High your dwelling place, there shall no evil befall you, nor any plague or calamity come near your tent. For He will give His angels [especial] charge over you to accompany and defend and preserve you in all your ways [of obedience and service]. They shall bear you up on their hands, lest you dash your foot against a stone. You shall tread upon the lion and adder; the young lion and the serpent shall you trample underfoot. Because he has set his love upon Me, therefore will I deliver him; I will set him on high, because he knows and understands My name [has a personal knowledge of My mercy, love, and kindness - trusts and relies on Me, knowing I will never forsake him, no, never]. He shall call upon Me, and I will answer him; I will be with him in trouble, I will deliver him and honor him. With long life will I satisfy him and show him My salvation.

Psalm 107:13-14

Then they cried to the Lord in their trouble, and He saved them out of their distresses. He brought them out of darkness and the shadow of death and broke apart the bonds that held them.

Psalm 107:20

He sends forth His word and heals them and rescues them from the pit and destruction.

Psalm 121:8

The Lord will keep your going out and your coming in from this time forth and forevermore.

Psalm 146:9

The Lord protects and preserves the strangers and temporary residents, He upholds the fatherless and the widow and sets them upright, but the way of the wicked He makes crooked (turns upside down and brings to ruin).

Proverbs 3:6

In all your ways know, recognize, and acknowledge Him, and He will direct and make straight and plain your paths.

Proverbs 3:23-24

Then you will walk in your way securely and in confident trust, and you shall not dash your foot or stumble. When you lie down, you shall not be afraid; yes, you shall lie down, and your sleep shall be sweet.

Proverbs 4:18

But the path of the [uncompromisingly] just and righteous is like the light of dawn, that shines more and more (brighter and clearer) until [it reaches its full strength and glory in] the perfect day [to be prepared].

Proverbs 5:2

That you may exercise proper discrimination and discretion and your lips may guard and keep knowledge and the wise answer [to temptation].

Proverbs 6:22

When you go, they [the words of your parents' God] shall lead you; when you sleep, they shall keep you; and when you waken, they shall talk with you.

Proverbs 10:3

The Lord will not allow the [uncompromisingly] righteous to famish, but He thwarts the desire of the wicked.

Proverbs 11:3a

The integrity of the upright shall guide them...

Proverbs 11:14

Where no wise guidance is, the people fall, but in the multitude of counselors there is safety.

Protection/Guidance

Proverbs 12:21

No [actual] evil, misfortune, or calamity shall come upon the righteous, but the wicked shall be filled with evil, misfortune, and calamity.

Proverbs 14:16

A wise man suspects danger and cautiously avoids evil, but the fool bears himself insolently and is [presumptuously] confident.

Proverbs 16:1

The plans of the mind and orderly thinking belong to man, but from the Lord comes the [wise] answer of the tongue.

Proverbs 16:3

Roll your works upon the Lord [commit and trust them wholly to Him; He will cause your thoughts to become agreeable to His will, and] so shall your plans be established and succeed.

Proverbs 16:9

A man's mind plans his way, but the Lord directs his steps and makes them sure.

Proverbs 16:33

The lot is cast into the lap, but the decision is wholly of the Lord [even the events that seem accidental are really ordered by Him].

Proverbs 19:21

Many plans are in a man's mind, but it is the Lord's purpose for him that will stand.

Romans 8:9

But you are not living the life of the flesh, you are living the life of the Spirit, if the [Holy] Spirit of God [really] dwells within you [directs and controls you]. But if anyone does not possess the [Holy] Spirit of Christ, he is none of His [he does not belong to Christ, is not truly a child of God].

1 Corinthians 2:16

For we have the mind of Christ (the Messiah) and do hold the thoughts (feelings and purposes) of His heart.

Protection/Guidance

5

FOR THE NATION

Psalm 7:9

Oh, let the wickedness of the wicked come to an end, but establish the uncompromisingly righteous [those upright and in harmony with You]; for You, who try the hearts and emotions and thinking powers, are a righteous God.

Psalm 16:1

Keep and protect me, O God, for in You I have found refuge, and in You do I put my trust and hide myself.

Psalm 34:1-7

I will bless the Lord at all times; His praise shall continually be in my mouth. My life makes its boast in the Lord; let the humble and afflicted hear and be glad. O magnify the Lord with me and let us exalt His name together. I sought (inquired of) the Lord and required Him [of necessity and on the authority of His Word], and He heard me, and delivered me from all my fears. They looked to Him and were radiant; their faces shall never blush for shame or be confused. This poor man cried, and the Lord heard him, and saved him out of all his troubles. The Angel of the Lord encamps around those who fear

Him [who revere and worship Him with awe] and each of them He delivers.

Psalm 35:1-6

Contend, O Lord, with those who contend with me; fight against those who fight against me! Take hold of shield and buckler and stand up for my help! Draw out also the spear and javelin and close up the way of those who pursue and persecute me. Say to me, I am your deliverance! Let them be put to shame and dishonor who seek and require my life; let them be turned back and confounded who plan my hurt! Let them be as chaff before the wind, with the Angel of the Lord driving them on! Let their way be through dark and slippery places, with the Angel of the Lord pursuing and afflicting them.

Psalm 54:1-7

Save me, O God, by Your name; judge and vindicate me by Your mighty strength and power. Hear my pleading and my prayer, O God; give ear to the words of my mouth. For strangers and insolent men are rising up against me, and violent men and ruthless ones seek and demand my life; they do not set God before them. Selah [pause, and calmly think of that]! Behold, God is my helper and ally; the Lord is my upholder and is with them who uphold my life. He will pay back evil to my enemies; in Your faithfulness [Lord] put an end to them. With a freewill offering I will sacrifice to You; I will give thanks and praise Your name, O Lord, for it is good. For He has delivered me out of every trouble, and my eye has looked [in triumph] on my enemies.

Psalm 141:8-10

But my eyes are toward You, O God the Lord; in You do I trust and take refuge; pour not out my life nor leave it destitute and bare. Keep me from the trap which they have laid for me, and the snares of evildoers. Let the wicked fall together into their own nets, while I pass over them and escape.

Isaiah 41:10-13

Fear not [there is nothing to fear], for I am with you; do not look around you in terror and be dismayed, for I am your God. I will strengthen and harden you to difficulties, yes, I will help you; yes, I will hold you up and retain you with My [victorious] right hand of rightness and justice. Behold, all they who are enraged and inflamed against you shall be put to shame and confounded; they who strive against you shall be as nothing and shall perish. You shall seek those who contend with you but shall not find them; they who war against you shall be as nothing, as nothing at all. For I the Lord your God hold your right hand; I am the Lord, who says to you, Fear not; I will help you!

Jeremiah 15:20-21

And I will make you to this people a fortified, bronze wall; they will fight against you, but they will not prevail over you, for I am with you to save and deliver you, says the Lord. And I will deliver you out of the hands of the wicked, and I will redeem you out of the palms of the terrible and ruthless tyrants.

Ephesians 2:10

For we are God's [own] handiwork (His workmanship), recreated in Christ Jesus, [born anew] that we may do those good works which God predestined (planned beforehand) for us [taking paths which He prepared ahead of time], that we should walk in them [living the good life which He prearranged and made ready for us to live].

2 Timothy 1:7

For God did not give us a spirit of timidity (of cowardice, of craven and cringing and fawning fear), but [He has given us a spirit] of power and of love and of calm and well-balanced mind and discipline and self-control.

⁓*Restore a Strong Economy*⁓

Deuteronomy 28:12-13

The Lord shall open to you His good treasury, the heavens, to give the rain of your land in its season and to bless all the work of your hands; and you shall lend to many nations, but you shall not borrow. And the Lord shall make you the head, and not the tail; and you shall be above only, and you shall not be beneath, if you heed the commandments of the Lord your God which I command you this day and are watchful to do them.

Psalm 35:27

Let those who favor my righteous cause and have pleasure in my uprightness shout for joy and be glad and say continually, Let the Lord be magnified, who takes pleasure in the prosperity of His servant.

Psalm 72:7

In His [Christ's] days shall the [uncompromisingly] righteous flourish and peace abound till there is a moon no longer.

Psalm 122:9

For the sake of the house of the Lord our God, I will seek, inquire for, and require your good.

Proverbs 8:17-18

I love those who love me, and those who seek me early and diligently shall find me. Riches and honor are with me, enduring wealth and righteousness (uprightness in every area and relation, and right standing with God).

Proverbs 13:21

Evil pursues sinners, but the consistently upright and in right standing with God is recompensed with good.

Proverbs 21:21

He who earnestly seeks after and craves righteousness, mercy, and loving-kindness will find life in addition to righteousness (uprightness and right standing with God) and honor.

Isaiah 48:17-18

Thus says the Lord, your Redeemer, the Holy One of Israel: I am the Lord your God, who teaches you to profit, who leads you in the way that you should go. O, that you had hearkened to My commandments! Then your peace and prosperity would have been like a flowing river, and your righteousness [the holiness and purity of the nation] like the [abundant] waves of the sea.

Jeremiah 32:15

For thus says the Lord of hosts, the God of Israel: Houses and fields and vineyards shall be purchased yet again in this land.

Jeremiah 33:9

And [Jerusalem] shall be to Me a name of joy, a praise and a glory before all the nations of the earth that hear of all the good I do for it, and they shall fear and tremble because of all the good and all the peace, prosperity, security, and stability I provide for it.

Zechariah 10:8

I will hiss for them [as the keeper does for his bees] and gather them in, for I have redeemed them, and they shall increase [again] as they have increased [before, in Egypt].

6

Pastors and Ministers

Proverbs 18:16

A man's gift makes room for him and brings him before great men.

Proverbs 20:5

Counsel in the heart of man is like water in a deep well, but a man of understanding draws it out.

Isaiah 54:17

But no weapon that is formed against you shall prosper, and every tongue that shall rise against you in judgment you shall show to be in the wrong. This [peace, righteousness, security, triumph over opposition] is the heritage of the servants of the Lord [those in whom the ideal Servant of the Lord is reproduced]; this is the righteousness or the vindication which they obtain from Me [this is that which I impart to them as their justification], says the Lord.

Matthew 10:40

He who receives you receives me, and he who receives me receives the one who sent me.

Mark 16:15

And He said to them, go into all the world and preach and publish openly the good news (the Gospel) to every creature [of the whole human race].

Luke 4:18

The Spirit of the Lord is on me, because he has anointed me to preach good news to the poor. He has sent me to proclaim freedom for the prisoners and recovery of sight for the blind, to release the oppressed.

Luke 4:32

And they were amazed at his teaching, for his word was with authority and ability and weight and power.

John 15:16 (NIV)

You did not choose me, but I chose you and appointed you to go and bear fruit - fruit that will last. Then the father will give you whatever you ask in my name.

Acts 1:8 (NIV)

But you will receive power when the Holy Spirit comes on you; And you will be my witnesses in Jerusalem, and in all Judea and Samaria, and to the ends of the earth.

Acts 4:29-30, 33 (NIV)

Now, Lord, consider their threats and enable your servants to speak your word with great boldness. Stretch out your hand to heal and perform miraculous signs and wonders through the name of your holy servant Jesus. With great power the apostles continued to testify to the resurrection of the Lord Jesus, and much grace was upon them all.

Acts 11:21 (NIV)

The Lord's hand was with them, and a great number of people believed and turned to the Lord.

Romans 4:20

No unbelief or distrust made him waver (doubtingly question) concerning the promise of God, but he grew strong and was empowered by faith as he gave praise and glory to God.

1 Corinthians 15:58

Therefore, my dear brothers, stand firm. Let nothing move you. Always give yourselves fully to the work of the Lord, because you know that your labor is not in vain.

2 Corinthians 2:14-17

But thanks be to God, who always leads us in triumphal procession in Christ and through US spreads everywhere the fragrance of the knowledge of him. For we are to God the aroma of Christ among those who are being saved and those who are perishing. To the one we are the smell of death; To the other, the fragrance of life. And who is equal to such a task? Unlike so many, we do not peddle the word of God for profit. On the contrary, in Christ we speak before God with sincerity, like men sent from God.

2 Corinthians 12:9-10 (NIV)

But he said to me, "my grace is sufficient for you, for my power is made perfect in weakness." therefore I will boast all the more gladly about my weaknesses, so that Christ power may rest on me. That is why, for Christ's sake, I delight and weakness, and insults, and hardships,

Pastors & Ministers

in persecutions, in difficulties. For when I am weak, then I am strong.

Ephesians 1:17-18

For I always pray to the God of our Lord Jesus Christ, the father of glory, that he may grant you a spirit of wisdom and revelation of insight into the mysteries and secrets in the deep and intimate knowledge of him; by having the eyes of your heart flooded with light, so that you can know and understand the hope to which he has called you, and how rich is his glorious inheritance in the saints (his set apart ones).

Ephesians 3:7-8 (NIV)

I became a servant of this gospel by the gift of God's grace given me through the working of his power. Although I am less than the least of all God's people, this grace was given me: to preach to the gentiles the unsearchable riches of Christ.

Ephesians 3:16-19

May he grant you out of the rich treasury of his glory to be strengthened and reinforced with mighty power in the inner man by the Holy Spirit [himself indwelling your innermost being and personality]. May Christ through your faith actually dwell (settle down, abide, make his permanent home) in your hearts! May you be rooted deep in love and found it securely on love. That you may have the power and be strong to apprehend and grasp with all the Saints [God's devoted people, the experience of that love] what is the breadth and length and height and depth of it. That you may really come to know [practically, through experience for yourselves] the love of Christ, which far surpasses mere knowledge without experience; that you may be filled [through all your being] unto all the fullness of God [may have the richest measure of the divine presence, and become a body wholly filled and flooded with God himself]!

Ephesians 4:11-12

And his gifts were [varied; He himself appointed and gave men to us] some to be apostles (special messengers), some prophets (inspired preachers and expounders) some evangelists (preachers of the gospel, traveling missionaries), some pastors (shepherds of his flock) and teachers. His intention was the perfecting and the full equipping of the saints (his consecrated people, that they should do the work of ministering towards building up Christ's body (the church).

Ephesians 4:15

Let our lives lovingly express truth [in all things, speaking truly, dealing truly, living truly]. enfolded in love, let us grow up in every way and in all things into him who is the head, even Christ (the Messiah, the Anointed One).

Ephesians 5:15-17 (NIV)

Be very careful, then, how you live not as unwise but as wise, making the most of every opportunity, because the days are evil period therefore do not be foolish, but understand what the Lord's will is.

Philippians 1:9-11 (NIV)

And this is my prayer: that your love may abound more and more in knowledge and depth of insight, so that you may be able to discern what is best and may be pure and blameless until the day of Christ, filled with the fruit of righteousness that comes through Jesus Christ dash to the glory and praise of God.

Philippians 2:20 (NIV)

I have no one else like him who takes a genuine interest in your welfare.

Colossians 1:9-12

... that you may be filled with the full (deep and clear) knowledge of his will in all spiritual wisdom [in comprehensive insight into the ways and purposes of God] and in understanding and discernment of spiritual things; That you may walk (live and conduct yourselves) in a manner worthy of the Lord, fully pleasing to him and desiring to please him in all things, bearing fruit in every good work and steadily growing and increasing in and by the knowledge of God [with fuller, deeper, and clearer inside, acquaintance, and recognition].[We pray] that you may be invigorated and strengthened with all power according to the might of his glory, [to exercise] every kind of endurance and patience (perseverance and forbearance) with joy; Giving thanks to the father, who has qualified and made us fit to share the portion which is the inheritance of the saints (God's holy people) in the Light.

Colossians 1:3-6 (NIV)

We always thank God, the father of our Lord Jesus Christ, when we pray for you, because we have heard of your faith in Christ Jesus and of the love you have for all the saints – the faith and love that spring from the hope that is stored up for you and haven and that you have already heard about in the word of truth, the gospel that has come to you. All over the world this gospel is bearing fruit and growing, just as it has been doing among you since the day that you heard it and understood God's grace in all its truth.

Colossians 1:28 (BSB)

We proclaim him, admonishing and teaching everyone with all wisdom, so that we may present everyone perfect in Christ.

Colossians 3:16 (BSB)

Let the word of Christ dwell in you richly as you teach and admonish one another with all wisdom, and as you sing psalms, hymns and spiritual songs with gratitude in your hearts to God.

Colossians 4:2-6

Be earnest and unwearied and steadfast in your prayer life, being [both] alert and intent in your praying with thanksgiving. And at the same time pray for us also, that God may open a door to us for the word (the gospel), to proclaim the mystery concerning Christ (the Messiah) on account of which I am in prison; That I may proclaim it fully and make it clear [speak boldly and unfold that mystery], as is my duty. Behave yourselves wisely [living prudently and with discretion] and your relations with those of the outside world (the non-Christians), making the very most of the time and seizing (buying up) the opportunity. Let your speech at all times be gracious (pleasant and winsome), seasoned [as it were] with salt,

Pastors & Ministers

so that you may never be at a loss to know how you ought to answer anyone who puts a question to you.

1 Thessalonians 2:7-8

As apostles of Christ, we could have been a burden to you, but we were gentle among you, like a mother caring for her little children. We loved you so much that we were delighted to share with you not only the gospel of God but our lives as well, because you had become so dear to us.

1 Thessalonians 2:11-12 (NIV)

For you know that we dealt with each of you as a father deals with his own children, encouraging, comforting and urging you to live lives worthy of God, who calls you into his Kingdom and glory.

1 Thessalonians 5:12-13 (NIV)

Now we ask you, brothers, to respect those who work hard among you, who are over you in the Lord and who admonish you. Hold them in highest regard and love because of their work period live in peace with each other.

1 Timothy 6:11-12 (NIV)

But you, man of God, flee from all this, and pursue righteousness, godliness, faith, love, endurance and gentleness. Fight the good fight of the faith. Take hold of the eternal life to which you were called when you made your good confession in the presence of many witnesses.

2 Timothy 2:15(NIV)

Do your best to present yourself to God as one approved, a workman who does not need to be ashamed and who correctly handles the word of truth.

Hebrews 4:12

For the word that God speaks is alive and full of power [making it active, operative, energizing, and effective]; it is sharper than any two-edged sword, penetrating to the dividing line of the breath of life (soul) and [the immortal] spirit, and of joints and marrow [of the deepest parts of our nature], exposing and sifting and analyzing and judging the very thoughts and purposes of the heart.

1 Peter 1:13

Therefore, prepare your minds for action; be self-controlled; Set your hope fully on the grace to be given you when Jesus Christ is revealed.

1 Peter 3:12

For the eyes of the Lord are upon the righteous (those who are upright and in right standing with God), and his ears are attentive to their prayer. But the face of the Lord is against those who practice evil [to oppose them, to frustrate, and defeat them].

1 John 2:20-21, 2: 24-27

But you have been anointed by [you hold a sacred appointment from, you have been given an unction from] the holy one, and you know all the truth or you know all things. I write to you not because you are ignorant and do not perceive and know the truth, but because you do perceive and know it, and know positively that nothing false (no deception, no lie) is of the truth. As for you, keep in your hearts what you have heard from the beginning. If what you have heard from the first dwells and remains in you, then you will dwell in the Son and in the father always. And this is what he himself has promised us - the life, the eternal life. I write this to you with reference to those who would deceive you, seduce and lead you astray. But as for you, the anointing (the sacred appointment, the unction) which you received from him abides permanently in you; so, then you have no need that anyone should instruct you. But just as his anointing teaches you concerning everything and is true and is no falsehood, so you must abide in (live in, never depart from) him [being rooted in him, knit to him], just as his anointing has taught you to do.

Revelation 3:8

I know your [record of] works and what you are doing. See! I have set before you a door wide open which no one is able to shut; I know that you have but little power, and yet you have kept my word and guarded my message and have not renounced or denied my name.

7

CHURCH GROWTH

Job 8:7

And though your beginning was small, yet your latter end would greatly increase.

Acts 2:42(NIV)

They devoted themselves to the apostles teaching and to the fellowship, to the breaking of bread and to prayer.

Acts 2:47

…and the Lord added to their number daily those who were being saved.

Acts 4:4

…many of those who heard the message believed (adhere to and trusted in and relied on Jesus as the Christ). And their number grew and came to about 5,000.

Acts 5:12(a)

Now by the hands of the apostles (special messengers) numerous and startling signs and wonders were being performed among the people.

Acts 5:14

More and more there were being added to the Lord those who believed [those who acknowledged Jesus as their savior and devoted themselves to him joined and gathered with them], crowds both of men and of women.

Acts 5:16

And the people gathered also from the towns and Hamlets around _____ (Jerusalem), bringing the sick and those troubled with foul spirits, and they were all cured.

Acts 5:42

Yet in spite of the threats, they never ceased for a single day, both in the temple area and at home, to teach and to proclaim the good news (Gospel) of Jesus [as] the Christ (the Messiah).

Acts 6:7

And the message of God kept on spreading, and the number of disciples multiplied greatly in _____ (Jerusalem)...

Acts 6:10

But they were not able to resist the intelligence and the wisdom and [the inspiration of] the Spirit with which and by whom _____ speaks.

Acts 8:6

And great crowds of people with one accord listened to and heeded what was said by _____, as they heard him and watched the miracles and wonders which he kept performing from time to time.

Acts 8:7

For foul spirits came out of many who were possessed by them, screaming and shouting with a loud voice, and many who were suffering from the palsy or were crippled were restored to health.

Acts 8:12

But when they believe the good news (the Gospel) about the Kingdom of God and the name of Jesus Christ (the Messiah) as _____ preached it, they were baptized, both men and women.

Acts 9:31

So, the church throughout the whole of _____ had peace and was edified [growing in wisdom, virtue, and piety] and walking in the respect and reverential fear of the Lord and in consolation and exhortation of the Holy Spirit, continued to increase and was multiplied.

Acts 16:4-5(NIV)

As they traveled from town to town, they delivered the decisions reached by the apostles and elders in Jerusalem for the people to obey. So, the churches were strengthened in the faith and grew daily in numbers.

8

SALVATION

Job 22:30

He will even deliver the one (for whom you intercede) who is not innocent; yes, he will be delivered through the cleanness of your hands.

Jeremiah 31:33-34

But this is the covenant which I will make with the House of Israel: after those days, says the Lord, I will put my law within them, and on their hearts will I write it; and I will be their God, and they will be my people. And they will know more teach each man his neighbor and each man his brother, saying, "Know the Lord," for they will all know me [recognize, understand, and be acquainted with me], from the least of them to the greatest, says the Lord. For I will forgive their iniquity, and I will [seriously] remember their sin no more.

John 1:12

But to as many as did receive and welcome him, he gave the authority (power, privilege, right) to become the children of God, that is, to those who believe in (and hereto, trust in, and rely on) His name.

Matthew 9:37-38

...The harvest is indeed plentiful, but the laborers are few. So pray to the Lord of the harvest to force out and thrust laborers into His harvest.

Matthew 12:29

How can a person go into a strong man's house and carry off his goods (the entire equipment of his house) without first binding the strong man? Then indeed he may plunder his house.

Luke 19:10

For the son of man came to seek and to save that which was lost.

Acts 3:19

So, repent (change your mind and purpose); turn around and return [to God], that your sins may be erased (blotted out, wiped clean), that times of refreshing (of recovering from the effects of heat, of reviving with fresh air) may come from the presence of the Lord.

Acts 4:12

And there is salvation in and through no one else, for there is no other name under heaven given among men by and in which we must be saved.

Acts 16:31

...Believe in the Lord Jesus Christ - of yourself up to him, take yourself out of your own keeping and entrust yourself into his keeping and you will be saved, and this applies both to you and your household as well.

Romans 10:9-10

If acknowledge and confess with your lips that Jesus is Lord and, in your heart, believe (adhere too, trust in, and rely on the truth) that God raised him from the dead, you will be saved. For with the heart a person believes (and adheres, trusts in, and relies on Christ) and so is justified (declared righteous, acceptable to God), and with the mouth he confesses (declares openly and speaks out freely his faith) and confirms his salvation.

2 Corinthians 4:4

For the God of this world has blinded the unbelievers' minds that they should not discern the truth, preventing them from seeing the illuminating light of the gospel of the glory of Christ (the Messiah), who is the image and likeness of God.

2 Corinthians 5:17

Therefore, if any person is [engrafted] in Christ (the Messiah) he is a new creation (a new creature altogether); the old [previous moral and spiritual condition] has passed away. Behold, the fresh and new has come!

Ephesians 1:17-18

For I always pray to the God of our Lord Jesus Christ, the father of glory, that he may grant you a spirit of wisdom and revelation of insight into mysteries and secrets in the deep and intimate knowledge of him, by having the eyes of your heart flooded with light, so that you can know and understand the hope to which he has called you, and how rich is his glorious inheritance in the saints (His set apart ones).

Salvation

Ephesians 2:8

For it is by free grace God's unmerited favor that you are saved delivered from judgment and made partakers of Christ's salvation through your faith. And this salvation is not of yourselves of your own doing, it came not through your own striving, but it is the gift of God.

2 Timothy 2:26

…that they may come to their senses and escape out of the snare of the devil, having been held captive by him, henceforth to do God's will.

Hebrews 8:12

For I will be merciful and gracious toward their sins, and I will remember their deeds of unrighteousness no more.

1 John 1:9

If we freely admit that we have sinned and confess our sins, he is faithful and just true to his own nature and promises and will forgive our sins dismiss our lawlessness and continuously cleanse us from all unrighteousness-everything not in conformity to his will in purpose, thought, and action.

Revelation 3:20

Behold, I stand at the door and knock; if anyone hears and listens to and heeds my voice and opens the door, I will come into him and will eat with him, and he will eat with me.

9

BACKSLIDERS

Psalm 51:10-12

> Create in me a clean heart, O God, and renew a right, preserving, and steadfast spirit within me. Cast me not away from your presence and take not your Holy Spirit from me. Restore to me the joy of your salvation and uphold me with a willing spirit.

Isaiah 57:18

> I have seen his willful ways, but I will heal him; I will lead him also and will recompense him and restore comfort to him and to those who mourn for him.

Jeremiah 31:11

> For the Lord has ransomed _____ and has redeemed him from the hand of him who was too strong for him.

Jeremiah 31:16-17

> Thus says the Lord: restrain your voice from weeping and your eyes from tears, for your work shall be rewarded, says the Lord; And your children shall return from the enemy's land. And there is hope for your future, says the Lord; Your children shall come back to their own country.

John 5:24

I assure you, most solemnly I tell you, the person whose ears are open to my words, who listens to my message, and believes and trusts in and clings to and relies on him whose sent me has, possesses now, eternal life. And he does not come into judgment. He does not incur sentence of judgment, will not come under condemnation, but he has already passed over out of death into life.

John 6:37

All whom my father gives and entrusts to me will come to me; And the one who comes to me I will most certainly not cast out. I will never, no never, reject one of them who comes to me.

John 6:45

It is written in the book of the prophets, and they shall I'll be taught of God, have him in person for their teacher. Everyone who has listened to and learned from my father comes to me.

John 10:28

And I give them eternal life, and they shall never lose it or perish throughout the ages period to all eternity they shall never by any means be destroyed. And no one is able to snatch them out of my hand.

Acts 3:19

So repent change your mind and purpose; Turn around and return to God, that your sins may be erased, blotted out, wiped clean, that times of refreshing, of recovering from the effects of heat, of reviving with fresh air may come from the presence of the Lord.

Romans 8:35-39

Who shall ever separate us from Christ's love? shall suffering and affliction and tribulation? Or calamity and distress? Or persecution or hunger or destitution or peril or sword? Even as it is written, "For Thy sake we are put to death all the day long; We are regarded and counted as sheep for the slaughter." Yet amid all these things we are more than conquerors and gain a surpassing victory through him who loved us. For I am persuaded beyond doubt, I am sure, that neither death nor life, nor angels, nor principalities, nor things impending and threatening nor things to come, nor powers, nor height, nor depth, nor anything else in all creation will be able to separate us from the love of God which is in Christ Jesus our Lord.

2 Timothy 2:26

… And that they may come to their senses and escape out of the snare of the devil, having been held captive by him, henceforth to do His, God's, will.

1 John 5:16

If anyone sees his brother believer committing a sin that does not lead to death, the extinguishing of life, he will pray, and God will give him life. Yes, he will grant life to all those whose sin is not leading one to death…

10

God's Will

Psalm 40:8

I delight to do your will, O my God; Yes, your law is within my heart.

Psalm 63:8

My whole being follows hard after you and clings closely to you; Your right hand upholds me.

John 5:30

I am able to do nothing from myself - independently, of my own accord but only as I am taught by God and as I get his orders. Even as I hear, a judge. I decide as I am bidden to decide. As the voice comes to me, so I give a decision, and my judgment is right, just, righteous, because I do not seek or consult my own will. I have no desire to do what is pleasing to myself, my own aim, my own purpose but only the will and pleasure of the father who sent me.

Acts 22:14

And he said, the God of our forefathers has destined and appointed you to come progressively to know his will, to perceive, to recognize more strongly and clearly, and to become better and more intimately acquainted with his will, and to see the righteous one, Jesus Christ, the Messiah, and to hear a voice from his own mouth and a message from his own lips.

Romans 6:18

And having been set free from sin, you have become the servants of righteousness (of conformity to the divine will in thought, purpose, and action).

1 Corinthians 2:10

...For the Holy Spirit searches diligently, exploring and examining everything, even sounding the profound and bottomless things of God [the divine counsels and things hidden and beyond man's scrutiny].

1 Corinthians 2:16

We have the mind of Christ (the Messiah) and to hold the thoughts (feelings and purposes) of his heart.

Ephesians 3:10

[The purpose is] that through the church the complicated, many-sided wisdom of God in all its infinite variety and innumerable aspects might now be made known to the angelic rulers and authorities (principalities and powers) in the heavenly sphere.

Ephesians 4:23-24

And be constantly renewed in the spirit of your mind [having a fresh mental and spiritual attitude] and put on the new nature (the regenerate self) created in God's image, [Godlike] in true righteousness and holiness.

Ephesians 5:15-16

Look carefully then how you walk! Live purposely and worthily and accurately, not as the unwise and witless, but as wise (sensible, intelligent people), making the very most of the time.

Philippians 1:9-10

And this I pray: that your love may abound yet more and more and extend to its fullest development in knowledge and all keen insight [that your love may display itself in greater depth of acquaintance and more comprehensive discernment], so that you may surely learn to sense what is the vital, and approve and prize what is excellent and of real value [recognizing the highest and the best, and distinguishing the moral differences], and that you may be untainted and pure and unerring and blameless [so that with heart sincere and certain and unsullied, you may approach] the day of Christ not stumbling nor causing others to stumble.

Colossians 1:9-1

...that you may be filled with the full (deep and clear) knowledge of his will in all spiritual wisdom [incomprehensive insight into the ways and purposes of God] and in understanding and discernment of spiritual things — that you may walk (live and conduct yourselves) in a manner worthy of the Lord, fully pleasing to him and desiring to please him in all things, bearing fruit in every good work and steadily growing and increasing in and by

God's Will

the knowledge of God [with fuller, deeper, and clearer insight, acquaintance, and recognition]. [We pray] that you may be invigorated and strengthened with all power according to the might of his glory, [to exercise] every kind of endurance and patience (perseverance and forbearance) with joy.

1 Peter 4:1-2

So, since Christ suffered in the flesh for us, for you, arm yourselves with the same thought and purpose [patiently to suffer rather than fail to please God]. for whoever has suffered in the flesh [having the mind of Christ] is done with intentional sin [has stopped pleasing himself and the world, and pleases God], so that he can no longer spend the rest of his natural life living by his human appetites and desires, but he lives for what God wills.

1 John 2:17

And the world passes away and disappears, and with it the forbidden cravings, the passionate desires, the lust of it; but he who does the will of God and carries out his purposes in his life abides, remains, forever.

11

~~~
∿
~~~

HARMONY IN MARRIAGE

Proverbs 5:15-19

Father, I pray and believe that _____ and I drink waters out of our own cistern [of a pure marriage relationship], and fresh running waters out of our own well. _____ confines himself to me alone and our children will be for us alone, and not the children of strangers with us. Are fountain of human life will be blessed [with the rewards of fidelity], and we rejoice in each other period I pray that I will be as the loving hind and pleasant doe [tender, gentle, attractive] -my bosom satisfies _____ at all times, and he will always be transported with delight in my love.

Jeremiah 17:7-18

I believe that we will be most blessed because we believe in, trust and, and rely on you, Lord, in whom our hope and confidence is-that we shall be as trees planted by the waters, that spread out their roots by the river and shall not see and fear when heat comes, but our leaves shall be green. We won't be anxious or "care"-ful in the year of drought nor cease from yielding fruit.

Jeremiah 32:39

> Thank you, Father, give us one heart and one way that we may fear you forever, for our good and for the good of our children after us.

Romans 13:13

> Let us live and conduct ourselves honorably and becomingly as in the [open light of] day, not in reveling (carousing) and drunkenness, not in immorality and debauchery (sensuality and licentiousness), not in quarreling and jealousy.

Romans 15:5-7

> Now may the God who gives the power of patient endurance (steadfastness) and who supplies encouragement, grant _____ and me to live in such mutual harmony and such full sympathy with one another, in accord with Christ Jesus, that together we may unanimously with united hearts and one voice, praise and glorify the God and the father of our Lord Jesus Christ (the Messiah); and that we welcome and receive one another, then, even as Christ has welcomed and received us, for the glory of God.

1 Corinthians 13:4-8

> I pray that our love endures long and is patient and kind; Our love is never envious nor boils over with jealousy; It is not boastful or vainglorious, does not display itself haughtily. Our love is not conceited (arrogant and inflated with pride); we are not rude (unmannerly) and do not act unbecomingly. God's love in us does not insist on its own rights or its own way, we are not self-seeking; we are not touchy or fretful or resentful; We take no

account and pay no attention to a suffered wrong. I pray that we would not rejoice at injustice and unrighteousness, but we do rejoice when right and truth prevail. Our love bears up under anything and everything that comes and is ever ready to believe the best of every person, its hopes are fadeless under all circumstances, and endures everything without weakening. Our love never fails and God's love in us never fades out or becomes obsolete or comes to an end.

Ephesians 4:31-32

Let all bitterness and indignation and wrath (passion, rage, bad temper) and resentment (anger, animosity) and quarreling (brawling, clamor, contention) and slander (evil speaking, abusive or blasphemous language) be banished from you, with all malice (spite, ill will, or baseness of any kind). and become useful and helpful and kind to one another, tender hearted (compassionate, understanding, loving hearted), forgiving one another [readily and freely], as God in Christ forgave you.

Ephesians 5:33

I pray that _____ will love me as his wife as being in a sense his very own self, and that I do respect, and reverence my husband and notice him, regard him, honor him, and prefer him, venerate and esteem him, that I defer to him, praise him, love and admire _____ exceedingly.

Philippians 1:27

I pray that _____ and I may stand firm in the united spirit and purpose, striving side by side and contending with a single mind for the faith of the glad tidings of the gospel.

Marriage

Colossians 2:2

I pray that _____ and my heart may be braced and comforted, cheered, and encouraged as we are knit together in love that we may come to have all the abounding wealth and blessing of assured conviction of understanding and that we may become progressively, more intimately acquainted with, and may know more definitely and accurately and thoroughly that mystic secret of God which is in Christ, the anointed one.

James 1:17-18

Father, I receive _____ as a gift, and I believe your word that every good and perfect, free, full gift is from above; It comes down from the father of all light, in the shining of whom there can be no variation, rising, or setting, or shadow cast by his turning; And it was of your own free will, that you gave us birth as sons by your word of truth, so that we should be a kind of first fruits of your creatures-a sample of what you created to be consecrated to yourself.

1 Peter 3:7

In the same way you married men should live considerately with [your wives], with an intelligent recognition [of the marriage relation], honoring the woman as [physically] the weaker, but [realizing that you] our joint heirs of the grace (God's unmerited favor) of life, in order that your prayers may not be hindered and cut off. [Otherwise, you cannot pray effectively.]

12

⟋⟍

My Mate

Psalm 37:23-24

The steps of a [good] man are directed and established by the Lord when he delights in his way [and he busies himself with his every step]. though he falls, he shall not be utterly cast down, for the Lord grasps his hand in support and upholds him.

Proverbs 2:10-16

For skillful and godly wisdom shall enter into _____'s heart, and knowledge shall be pleasant to _____. Discretion shall watch over _____, understanding shall keep _____, to deliver _____ from the way of evil and the evil men, for men who speak perverse things in our liars, men who forsake the paths of brightness to walk in the ways of darkness, who rejoiced to do evil and delight in the perverseness of evil, who are crooked in their ways, wayward and devious in their paths. [Discretion shall watch over_____, understanding shall keep _____] to deliver _____ from the alien woman, from the outsider with her flattering words.

Proverbs 3:26

For the Lord shall be _____'s confidence, firm and strong, and shall keep _____'s foot from being caught [in a trap or some hidden danger].

Proverbs 4:8

_____ prizes this wisdom highly and exalts her, and she exalts and promotes_____, she will bring _____ to honor when _____ embraces her.

Proverbs 8:6-8

Hear, for _____ will speak excellent and princely things; And the opening of _____'s lips shall be for right things. For _____'s mouth shall utter truth, and wrongdoing is detestable and loathsome to _____'s lips. All the words of _____mouth our righteous (upright and in right standing with God); there is nothing contrary to truth or crooked in them.

Proverbs 10:6

Blessings are upon the head of _____, the uncompromisingly righteous (the upright, in right standing with God).

Proverbs 11:16

A gracious and good woman wins honor for her husband...

Proverbs 12:4

A virtuous and worthy wife [earnest and strong in character] is a crowning joy to her husband...

Proverbs 12:14

From the fruit of his words _____shall be satisfied with good, and the work of ____'s hands shall come back to him [as a harvest].

Proverbs 13:20-21

He who walks [as a companion] with wise men is wise… the consistently upright and in right standing with God is recompensed with good.

Proverbs 14:16

_____ is a wise man who suspects danger and cautiously avoids evil…

Proverbs 18:16

_____'s gift makes room for him and brings him before great men.

Proverbs 19:14

… A wise, understanding, and prudent wife is from the Lord.

Proverbs 19:22

_____ has that which is desired in a man-loyalty and kindness-and his glory and delight are his giving.

Proverbs 21:5

The thoughts of_____, the [steadily] diligent, tend only to plenteousness…

Mate

Proverbs 24:14

So _____ has known skillful and godly wisdom to be sweet to his life. _____ has found it, so there shall be a future and a reward, and _____'s hope and expectations shall not be cut off.

Proverbs 31:11

The heart of her husband's trust in her confidently and relies on and believes in her securely, so that he has no lack of [honest] gain or need of [dishonest] spoil.

Proverbs 31:23

Her husband is known in the [city's] gates, when he sits among the elders of the land.

Song of Solomon 5:10-16

[She said] My beloved is fair and ruddy, the chief among ten thousand! His head is [as precious as] the finest gold; his locks are curly and bushy and black as a raven. His eyes are like doves beside the water brooks, bathed in milk and fitly set. His cheeks are like a bed of spices or balsam, like banks of sweet herbs yielding fragrance. His lips are like bloodred anemones or lilies distilling liquid [sweet-scented] myrrh. His hands are like rods of gold set with [nails of] beryl or topaz. His body is a figure of bright ivory overlaid with [veins of] sapphires. His legs are like strong and steady pillars of marble set upon bases of fine gold. His appearance is like Lebanon, excellent, stately, and majestic as the cedars. His voice and speech are exceedingly sweet; yes, he is altogether lovely [the whole of him delights and is precious]. This is my beloved, and this is my friend, O daughters of Jerusalem!

Song of Solomon 7:10

I am my beloved's, and his desire is toward me.

Song of Solomon 8:7

Many waters cannot quench love, neither can floods drown it.

Isaiah 48:17

Thus says the Lord, your Redeemer, the holy one of Israel: I am the Lord your God, who teaches _____ to profit, who leads _____ in the way that he should go.

Colossians 3:16

_____ lets the word [spoken by] Christ (the Messiah) have its home [in his heart and mind] and [the word] dwells in _____ in [all its] richness, as _____ teaches and admonishes and trains one another in all insight and intelligence and wisdom [in spiritual things, and sings] psalms and hymns and spiritual songs making melody to God with his grace in _____'s heart.

1 Peter 3:2-6

When they observed the pure and modest way in which you conduct yourselves, together with your reverence [for your husband; You are to feel for him all that reverence includes: to respect, defer to, revere him-to honor, esteem, appreciate, prize, and, in the human sense, to adore him, that is, to admire, praise, be devoted to, deeply love, and enjoy your husband]. Let not yours be the merely external adorning with elaborate interweaving and knotting of the hair, the wearing of jewelry, are changes of clothes; But let it be the inward adorning and beauty of the hidden person

Mate

of the heart, with the incorruptible and unfading charm of a gentle and peaceful spirit, which [is not anxious or wrought up, but] is very precious in the sight of God. For it was thus that the pious woman of old who hoped in God were [accustomed] to beautify themselves and were submissive to their husbands [adapting themselves to them as themselves secondary independent upon them]. It was thus that Sarah obeyed Abraham [following his guidance and acknowledging his leadership over her by] calling him Lord (master, leader, authority). And you are now her true daughters if you do right and let nothing terrify you [not giving way to hysterical fears or letting anxieties unnerve you].

13

CHILDREN

Psalm 1:3

...everything he does shall proper [and come to maturity].

Psalm 92:10-14

My horn (emblem of excessive strength and stately grace) You have exalted like that of a wild ox; I am anointed with fresh oil. My eye looks upon those who lie and wait for me... the uncompromisingly righteous shall flourish like the palm tree [be long lived, stately, upright, useful, and fruitful]; they shall grow like a cedar in Lebanon... [Growing in grace] they shall still bring forth fruit in old age; they shall be full of sap [of spiritual vitality...

Psalm 113:9(KJV)

He makes the barren woman to keep house, and to be joyful mother of children. Praise ye the Lord.

Psalm 127:3-4

Behold, children are a heritage from the Lord, the fruit of the womb a reward. As arrows are in the hand of a warrior, so are the children of one's youth.

Psalm 128:3

Your wife shall be like a fruitful vine in the innermost parts of your house; Your children shall be like olive plants round about your table.

Jeremiah 17:8

For he shall be like a tree planted by the waters that spreads out its roots by the river; and it shall not see and fear when heat comes; But its leaf shall be green. It shall not be anxious and full of care in the year of drought, nor shall it cease yielding fruit.

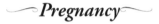

Pregnancy

Genesis 49:25

By the God of your father, who will help you, and by the Almighty, who will bless you with blessings of the heavens above, blessings lying in the deep beneath, blessings of the breasts and of the womb.

Exodus 23:26

(Prevent miscarriage and premature birth) None shall lose her young by miscarriage or be barren in your land; I will fulfill the number of your days.

Deuteronomy 7:13

And He will love you, bless you, and multiply you; He will also bless the fruit of your body...

Deuteronomy 32:4

He is the Rock, his work is perfect, for all His ways are law and justice. A God of faithfulness without breach or deviation, just and right is He.

Psalm 57:2

I will cry to God Most High, who performs on my behalf and rewards me [Who brings to pass His purposes for me and surely completes them].

Psalm 138:8

The Lord will perfect that which concerns me…

Psalm 147:13

For He has strengthened and made hard the bars of your gates, and He has blessed your children within you.

Isaiah 44:2

Thus says the Lord, who made you and formed you from the womb, Who will help you…

Isaiah 44:24

Thus says the Lord, your Redeemer, and He Who formed you from the womb: I and the Lord, who made all things, Who alone stretched out the heavens, Who spread out the earth by Myself [who was with Me]?

Isaiah 49:1

…The Lord has called me from the womb; From the body of my mother He has named my name.

Philippians 1:6

…He Who Began a good work in you will continue until the day of Jesus Christ [right up to the time of His return], developing [that good work] and perfecting and bringing it to full completion in you.

⁓*Childbirth*⁓

Exodus 1:19

The midwives answered Pharaoh, "because the Hebrew women are not like the Egyptian women; They are vigorous and quickly delivered; Their babies are born before the midwife comes to them."

Deuteronomy 28:6

Blessed shall you be when you come in and blessed shall you be when you go out.

Deuteronomy 28:13

(To prevent breech birth) And the Lord shall make you the head, and not the tail; And you shall be above only, and you shall not be beneath.

Psalm 4:1

Answer me when I call, O God of my righteousness (uprightness, justice, and right standing with You)! You have freed me when I was hemmed in and enlarged me when I was in distress; have mercy upon me and hear my prayer.

Psalm 22:9-10

Yet You are He Who took me out of the womb; You made me hope and trust when I was on my mother's breasts. I was cast upon You from my very birth; From my mother's womb You have been my God.

Psalm 57:2

I will cry to God Most High, Who performs on my behalf and rewards me [Who brings to pass His purposes for me and surely completes them].

Psalm 147:13

For He has strengthened and made hard the bars of your gates and He has blessed your children within you.

Isaiah 65:23

They shall not labor in vain or bring forth children for sudden terror or calamity; For they shall be the descendants of the blessed of the Lord, and their offspring with them.

Isaiah 66:7-9

Before [Zion] travailed, she gave birth; Before her pain came upon her, she was delivered of a male child. Who has heard of such a thing? Who has seen such things? Shall a land be born in one day? Or shall a nation be brought forth in a moment? For as soon as Zion was in labor, she brought forth her children." Shall I bring to the moment of birth and not cause to bring forth?" says the Lord. "Shall I Who Causes to bring forth shut the womb?" says your God.

Luke 1:42

And she cried out with a loud cry, and then exclaimed, "Blessed (favored of God) above all other women are you! And blessed (favored of God) is the fruit of your womb!"

1 Timothy 2:15

Notwithstanding, she shall be saved in childbearing, if they continue in faith and charity and holiness with sobriety.

2 Timothy 1:7

(To prevent tenseness that would cause pain) For God did not give us a spirit of timidity (of cowardice, of craven and

cringing and fawning fear) but [He has given us a spirit] of power and of love and of calm and well-balanced mind and discipline and self-control.

~Nursing~

Genesis 49:25

By the God of your father, who will help you, and by the Almighty, who will bless you with the blessings of the heavens above, blessings lying in the deep beneath, blessings of the breasts and of the womb.

Isaiah 66:11

That you may nurse and be satisfied from her consoling breast, that you may drink deeply and be delighted with the abundance and the brightness of her glory.

1 Peter 2:2

Like newborn babies you should crave (thirst for, earnestly desire) the pure (unadulterated) spiritual milk, that by it you may be nurtured...

~Children~

Psalm 103:17

But the mercy and loving kindness of the Lord are from everlasting to everlasting upon those who reverently and worshipfully fear Him, and his righteousness to children's children.

Psalm 112:2

His [spiritual] offspring shall be mighty upon the earth; The generation of the upright shall be blessed.

Psalm 127:3-5

Behold, children are a heritage from the Lord, the fruit of the womb a reward. As arrows are in the hand of a warrior, so are the children of one's youth. Happy, blessed, and fortunate is the man whose quiver is filled with them.

Proverbs 5:16-17

Should your offspring be dispersed abroad as water brooks in the streets? Confine yourself to your own wife; Let your children be for you alone, and not the children of strangers with you.

Proverbs 23:24-25

The father of the uncompromisingly righteous (the upright, and right standing with God) shall greatly rejoice, and he who becomes the father of a wise child shall have joy in him. Let your father and your mother be glad and let her who bore you rejoice.

Isaiah 29:22-23

For you shall not then be ashamed; Not then shall your face become pale with fear and disappointment because of your children's degeneracy. For when you see your children walking in the way of piety and virtue, the work of His hands in your midst, they will revere His name.

Isaiah 43:5

Fear not, for I am with you; I will bring your offspring from the east [where they are dispersed] and gather you from the west.

Isaiah 49:25

...for I will contend with him who contends with you, and I will give safety to your children and ease them.

Isaiah 54:13

All of my children shall be disciples, taught of the Lord, and great shall be their peace and undisturbed composure.

Isaiah 59:21

For this is the covenant that the Lord has made with me-His Spirit is upon me, who writes the law of God inwardly in my heart, and his words which he has put in my mouth shall not depart out of my mouth, or out of the mouth of my children, or out of the mouth of my children's children henceforth and forever.

Jeremiah 31:16

Thus says the Lord: restrain your voice from weeping and your eyes from tears, for your work shall be rewarded, says the Lord; And [your children] shall return from the enemy's land.

1 Thessalonians 2:7-8

But we behaved gently when we were among you, like a devoted mother tenderly caring for her own children. Having such a deep affection for you, we were delighted to share with you not only God's good news but also our own lives, because you had become so very dear to us.

Ephesians 6:1-2

Children, obey your parents in the Lord [that is, accept their guidance and discipline as His representatives], for this is right [for obedience teaches wisdom and self-discipline]. Honor [esteem, value as precious] your father and your mother [and be respectful to them]—this is the first commandment with a promise.

⟶*Child Raising*⟵

Proverbs 13:24

He who spares his rod [of discipline] hates his son, but he who loves him disciplines diligently and punishes him early.

Proverbs 19:18

Discipline your son while there is hope, but do not [indulge your angry resentments by undue chastisements and] set yourself to his ruin.

Proverbs 20:30

Blows that wound cleanse away evil, and strokes [for correction] reach to the innermost parts.

Proverbs 22:6

Train up a child in the way he should go [and in keeping with his individual gift or bent], and when he is old, he will not depart from it.

Proverbs 22:15

Foolishness is bound up in the heart of a child, but the rod of discipline will drive it far from him.

Proverbs 23:13-14

Withhold not discipline from the child; for if you strike and punish him with the [reedlike] rod, he will not die.

You shall whip him with the rod and deliver his life from Sheol (Hades, the place of the dead).

Proverbs 29:15, 17

The rod and reproof give wisdom, but a child left undisciplined brings his mother to shame. Correct your son, and he will give you rest; yes, he will give delight to your heart.

14

PROSPERITY

Joshua 1:8

This book of the law shall not depart out of your mouth, but you shall meditate on it day and night, that you may observe and do according to all that is written in it. For then shall you make your way prosperous, and then shall you deal wisely and have good success.

Psalm 1:3

And he shall be like a tree firmly planted [and tended] by the streams of water, ready to bring forth its fruit in its season; its leaf also shall not fade or wither; and everything he does shall prosper [and come to maturity].

Psalm 34:10

The young lions lack food and suffer hunger, but they who seek (inquire of and require) the Lord [by right of their need and on the authority of His Word], none of them shall lack any beneficial thing.

Psalm 37:25

I have been young and now am old, yet have I not seen the [uncompromisingly] righteous forsaken or their seed begging bread.

Psalm 104:28

When You give it to them, they gather it up; You open Your hand, and they are filled with good things.

Psalm 111:5

He has given food and provision to those who reverently and worshipfully fear Him; He will remember His covenant forever and imprint it [on His mind].

Psalm 112:1,3

Praise the Lord! (Hallelujah!) Blessed (happy, fortunate, to be envied) is the man who fears (reveres and worships) the Lord, who delights greatly in His commandments. Prosperity and welfare are in his house, and his righteousness endures forever.

Psalm 119:25

My earthly life cleaves to the dust; revive and stimulate me according to Your word!

Proverbs 3:9-10

Honor the Lord with your capital and sufficiency [from righteous labors] and with the first fruits of all your income; So, shall your storage places be filled with plenty, and your vats shall be overflowing with new wine.

Proverbs 10:4

He becomes poor who works with a slack and idle hand, but the hand of the diligent makes rich.

Proverbs 10:16

The earnings of the righteous (the upright, in right standing with God) lead to life, but the profit of the wicked leads to further sin.

Proverbs 10:22

The blessing of the Lord - it makes [truly] rich, and He adds no sorrow with it [neither does toiling increase it].

Proverbs 15:6

In the house of the [uncompromisingly] righteous is great [priceless] treasure, but with the income of the wicked is trouble and vexation.

Proverbs 24:3-4

Through skillful and godly Wisdom is a house (a life, a home, a family) built, and by understanding it is established [on a sound and good foundation].

Proverbs 28:19-20

He who cultivates his land will have plenty of bread, but he who follows worthless people and pursuits will have poverty enough. A faithful man shall abound with blessings, but he who makes haste to be rich [at any cost] shall not go unpunished.

Isaiah 48:17

...I am the Lord your God, who teaches you to profit, who lead you in the way that you should go.

Malachi 3:10

Bring all the tithes (the whole tenth of your income) into the storehouse, that there may be food in My house, and prove Me now by it, says the Lord of hosts, if I will not open the windows of heaven for you and pour you out a blessing, that there shall not be room enough to receive it.

Luke 6:38

Give, and [gifts] will be given to you; good measure, pressed down, shaken together, and running over, will they pour into [the pouch formed by] the bosom [of your robe and used as a bag]. For with the measure, you deal out [with the measure you use when you confer benefits on others], it will be measured back to you.

John 10:10

The thief comes only in order to steal and kill and destroy. I came that they may have and enjoy life, and have it in abundance (to the full, till it overflows).

2 Corinthians 8:9

For you are becoming progressively acquainted with and recognizing more strongly and clearly the grace of our Lord Jesus Christ (His kindness, His gracious generosity, His undeserved favor and spiritual blessing), [in] that though He was [so very] rich, yet for your sakes He became [so very] poor, in order that by His poverty you might become enriched (abundantly supplied).

2 Corinthians 9:6, 8

...[Remember] this: he who sows sparingly and grudgingly will also reap sparingly and grudgingly, and he who sows generously [that blessings may come to someone] will also reap generously and with blessings. And God is able to make all grace (every favor and earthly blessing) come to you in abundance, so that you may always and under all circumstances and whatever the need be self-sufficient [possessing enough to require no aid or support and furnished in abundance for every good work and charitable donation].

Galatians 3:13

Christ purchased our freedom [redeeming us] from the curse (doom) of the Law [and its condemnation] by [Himself] becoming a curse for us, for it is written [in the Scriptures], Cursed is everyone who hangs on a tree (is crucified).

Philippians 4:19

And my God will liberally supply (fill to the full) your every need according to His riches in glory in Christ Jesus.

1 Timothy 6:17-18

As for the rich in this world, charge them not to be proud and arrogant and contemptuous of others, nor to set their hopes on uncertain riches, but on God, who richly and ceaselessly provides us with everything for [our] enjoyment. [Charge them] to do good, to be rich in good works, to be liberal and generous of heart, ready to share [with others].

3 John 1:2

Beloved, I pray that you may prosper in every way and [that your body] may keep well, even as [I know] your soul keeps well and prospers.

15

Protection in the Home

Psalm 91:10

There shall no evil befall you, nor any plague or calamity come near your tent.

Psalm 122:7

May peace be within your walls and prosperity within your palaces!

Proverbs 1:33

But whoso hearkens to me [Wisdom] shall dwell securely and in confident trust and shall be quiet, without fear or dread of evil.

Proverbs 3:33

...He declares blessed (joyful and favored with blessings) the home of the just and consistently righteous.

Proverbs 12:7

The wicked are overthrown and are not, but the house of the uncompromisingly righteous shall stand.

Proverbs 15:6

In the house of the uncompromisingly righteous is great [priceless] treasure…

Proverbs 24:3-4

Through skillful and godly Wisdom is a house (a life, a home, a family) built, and by understanding it is established [on a sound and good foundation], and by knowledge shall its chambers [of every area] be filled with all precious and pleasant riches.

Proverbs 24:15

Lie not in wait as a wicked man against the dwelling of the uncompromisingly righteous (the upright, in right standing with God); destroy not his resting place. (*No vandalism*)

16

HEALING

Exodus 15:26

Saying, if you will diligently hearken to the voice of the Lord your God and will do what is right in His sight and will listen to and obey His commandments and keep all His statutes, I will put none of the diseases upon you which I brought upon the Egyptians, for I am the Lord Who heals you.

Exodus 23:25

(Stomach trouble and ulcers) You shall serve the Lord your God; He shall bless your bread and water, and I will take sickness from your midst.

Job 33:25

(Skin) [Then the man's] flesh shall be restored; It becomes fresher and more tender than a child's; He returns to the days of his youth.

Psalm 30:2

O Lord my God, I cried to You, and You have healed me.

Psalm 34:19

Many evils confront the consistently righteous, but the Lord delivers him out of them all.

Psalm 34:20

(Bones) He keeps all his bones; Not one of them is broken.

Psalm 41:3

The Lord will sustain, refresh, and strengthen him on his bed of languishing; All his bed you [O Lord] will turn, change, and transform in his illness.

Psalm 73:26

(Heart) My flesh and my heart may fail, but God is the rock and firm strength of my heart and my portion forever.

Psalm 91:10

(Protection from disease) There shall no evil befall you, nor any plague or calamity come near your tent.

Psalm 103:2-3

Bless (affectionately, gratefully praise) the Lord, O my soul, and forget not [one of] all His benefits - who forgives [every one of] all your iniquities, who heals [each one of] all your diseases.

Psalm 107:20

He sends forth his word and heals them and rescues them from the pit and destruction.

Psalm 118:17

I shall not die but live and shall declare the works and recount the illustrious acts of the Lord.

Psalm 146:3

Put not your trust in princes, and a son of man, in whom there is no help.

Psalm 146:8

(Blind, curvature of spine) The Lord opens the eyes of the blind, the Lord lifts up those who are bowed down, the Lord loves the uncompromisingly righteous (those upright in heart and in right standing with Him).

Proverbs 3:8

(Leukemia) It (the Word) shall be health to your nerves and sinews, and marrow and moistening to your bones.

Proverbs 3:26 KJV

(Amputation) For the Lord shall be the confidence and shall keep thy foot from being taken.

Proverbs 4:20-22

My son, attend to my words; Consent and submit to my sayings. Let them not depart from your side; Keep them in the center of your heart. For they are life to those who find them, healing and health to all their flesh.

Proverbs 14:30

A calm and undisturbed mind and heart are the life and health of the body, but envy, jealousy, and wrath are like rottenness of the bones.

Healing

Proverbs 15:4

A gentle tongue [with its healing power] is a tree of life, but willful contrariness in it breaks down the spirit.

Proverbs 17:22

A happy heart is good medicine and a cheerful mind works healing, but a broken spirit dries up the bones.

Proverbs 18:14

The strong spirit of a man's sustains him in bodily pain or trouble…

Proverbs 18:21

Death and life are in the power of the tongue, and they who indulge in it shall eat the fruit of it [for death or life].

Song of Solomon 6:6

(*Teeth*) Your teeth are like a flock of ewes coming from their washing, of which all are in pairs, and not one of them is missing.

Isaiah 29:18

(*Blind, deaf*) And in that day shall the deaf hear the words of the book, and out of obscurity and gloom and darkness the eyes of the blind shall see.

Isaiah 32:3

(*Eyesight*) The eyes of those who see will not be closed or dimmed, and the ears of those who hear will listen.

Isaiah 32:4

(Speech impediment) And the mind of the rash will understand knowledge and have good judgment, and the tongue of the stammerers will speak readily and plainly.

Isaiah 40:29

(Weak, faint) He gives power to the faint and weary, and to him who has no might He increases strength [causing it to multiply and making it to abound].

Isaiah 53:4-5

Surely, He has borne our griefs (sicknesses, weaknesses, and distresses) and carried our sorrows and pains [of punishment], yet we [ignorantly] considered Him stricken, smitten, and afflicted by God [as if with leprosy]. But He was wounded for our transgressions, He was bruised for our guilt and iniquities; the chastisement [needful to obtain] peace and well-being for us was upon Him, and with the stripes [that wounded] Him we are healed and made whole.

Isaiah 58:8

Then shall your light break forth like the morning, and your healing (your restoration and the power of a new life) shall spring forth speedily; your righteousness (your rightness, your justice, and your right relationship with God) shall go before you [conducting you to peace and prosperity], and the glory of the Lord shall be your rear guard.

Jeremiah 17:14

Heal me, O Lord, and I shall be healed; Save me, and I shall be saved, for you are my praise.

Jeremiah 30:17

For I will restore health to you, and I will heal your wounds, says the Lord…

Ezekiel 16:6

(Blood) And when I passed by you and saw you rolling about in your blood, I said to you in your blood, "Live!" yes, I said to you still in your natal blood, "Live!"

Joel 3:10

… let the weak say, "I am strong [a warrior]!"

Nahum 1:9 (KJV)

… affliction shall not rise up the second time.

Zephaniah 3:19

(Limping) Behold, at that time I will deal with all those who afflict you; I will save the limping [ones] and gather the outcast and we'll make them a praise and a name in every land of their shame.

Malachi 4:2

But unto you who revere and worshipfully fear my name shall the Son of Righteousness arise with healing in his wings and his beams, and you shall go forth and gambol like calves [released] from the stall and leap for joy.

Luke 6:19

All the multitude were seeking to touch him, for healing power was all the while going forth from him and curing them all [saving them from severe illnesses or calamities].

Acts 10:38

God anointed and consecrated Jesus of Nazareth with the [Holy] Spirit and with strength and ability and power; How He went about doing good and, in particular, curing all who were harassed and oppressed by [the power of] the devil, for God was with Him.

Galatians 3:13

Christ purchased our freedom [redeeming us] from the curse (doom) of the Law [and its condemnation] by [Himself] becoming a curse for us, for it is written [in the Scriptures], Cursed is everyone who hangs on a tree (is crucified).

Philippians 4:7

(Nerves) And God's peace [shall be yours, that tranquil state of a soul assured of its salvation through Christ, and so fearing nothing from God and being content with its earthly lot of whatever sort that is, that peace] which transcends all understanding shall garrison and mount guard over your hearts and minds in Christ Jesus.

Hebrews 4:12

(Arthritis) For the Word that God speaks is alive and full of power [making it active, operative, energizing and effective]; it is sharper than any two-edged sword, penetrating to the dividing line of the breath of life (soul) and [the immortal] spirit, and of the joints and marrow...

Hebrews 12:12-13

(Knees) So then, brace up and reinvigorate and set brought your slackened and weakened and drooping hands and strengthen your feeble and palsies and tottering knees, and cut through and make firm and plain and smooth, straight paths for your feet [yes, make them safe and upright and happy paths that go in the right direction], so that the lame and halting [limbs] may not be put out of joint, but rather be cured.

James 5:15

And the prayer [that is] our faith will save him who is sick, and the Lord will restore him; And if he has committed sins, he will be forgiven.

1 Peter 2:24

He personally bore our sins in His [own] body on the tree [as on an altar and offered Himself on it], that we might die (cease to exist) to sin and live to righteousness. By His wounds we have been healed.

17

WISDOM

Psalm 37:30

The mouth of the uncompromisingly righteous utters wisdom, and his tongue speaks with justice.

Proverbs 2:2-7

Making your ear attentive to skillful and godly Wisdom and inclining and directing your heart and mind to understanding [applying all your powers to the quest for it]; Yes, if you cry out for insight and raise your voice for understanding, If you seek [Wisdom] as for silver and search for skillful and godly Wisdom as for hidden treasures, Then you will understand the reverent and worshipful fear of the Lord and find the knowledge of [our omniscient] God. For the Lord gives skillful and godly Wisdom; from His mouth come knowledge and understanding. He hides away sound and godly Wisdom and stores it for the righteous (those who are upright and in right standing with Him); He is a shield to those who walk uprightly and in integrity.

Proverbs 2:10-11

For skillful and godly wisdom shall enter your heart, and knowledge shall be pleasant to you. Discretion shall watch over you, understanding shall keep you.

Proverbs 3:16-18

Length of days is in her right hand, and in her left hand are riches and honor. Her ways are highways of pleasantness, and all her paths are peace. She is a tree of life to those who lay hold on her; and happy (blessed, fortunate, to be envied) is everyone who holds her fast.

Proverbs 3:23-24

Then you will walk in your way securely and in confident trust, and you shall not dash your foot or stumble. When you lie down, you shall not be afraid; Yes, you shall lie down, and your sleep shall be sweet.

Proverbs 4:6-8

Forsake not [Wisdom], and she will keep, defend, and protect you; love her, and she will guard you. The beginning of Wisdom is: get Wisdom (skillful and godly Wisdom)! [For skillful and godly Wisdom is the principal thing.] And with all you have gotten, get understanding (discernment, comprehension, and interpretation). Prize Wisdom highly and exalt her, and she will exalt and promote you; she will bring you to honor when you embrace her.

Proverbs 5:2

That you may exercise proper discrimination and discretion and your lips may guard and keep knowledge and the wise answer [to temptation].

Proverbs 8:11

For skillful and godly wisdom is better than rubies or pearls, and all the things that may be desired are not to be compared with it.

Proverbs 8:18

Riches and honor are with me, enduring wealth and righteousness (up brightness in every area and relation, and right standing with God).

Proverbs 8:21

That I may cause those who love me to inherit [true] riches and that I may fill their treasures.

Proverbs 9:11

For by me [wisdom from God] your days shall be multiplied, and the years of your life shall be increased.

Proverbs 12:18

... the tongue of the wise brings healing.

Proverbs 16:1

The plans of the mind and orderly thinking belong to man, but from the Lord comes the [wise] answer of the tongue.

Proverbs 16:3

Roll your works upon the Lord [commit and trust them wholly to Him; He will cause your thoughts to become agreeable to His will, and] so shall your plans be established and succeed.

Proverbs 17:27

He who has knowledge spares his words, and a man of understanding has a cool spirit.

Proverbs 18:4

The words of a [discreet and wise] man's mouth are like deep waters [plenteous and difficult to fathom], and the fountain of skillful and godly wisdom is like a gushing stream [sparkling, fresh, pure, and life-giving].

Proverbs 24:14

So shall you know skillful and godly wisdom to be thus to your life; If you find it, then shall there be a future and a reward, and your hope and expectation shall not be cut off.

Isaiah 33:6

There shall be stability in your times, an abundance of salvation, wisdom, and knowledge; The reverent fear and worship of the Lord is your treasure and His.

Mark 4:22

Things are hidden temporarily only as a means to revelation. For there is nothing hidden except to be revealed, nor is anything [temporarily] kept secret except in order that it may be made known.

Luke 21:15

For I [Myself] we'll give you a mouth and such utterance and wisdom that all of your foes combined will be unable to stand against or refute.

1 Corinthians 1:24

But to those who are called, whether Jew or Greek (Gentile), Christ [is] the Power of God and the wisdom of God.

1 Corinthians 1:30

But it is from him that you have your life in Christ Jesus, whom God made our wisdom from God, [revealed to us a knowledge of the divine plan of salvation previously hidden, manifesting itself as] our righteousness [thus making us upright and putting us in right standing with God], and our consecration [making us pure and holy], and our redemption [providing our ransom from eternal penalty for sin].

Ephesians 1:8

He lavished upon us in every kind of wisdom and understanding (practical insight and prudence).

Ephesians 1:17

I pray to the God of our Lord Jesus Christ, the Father of glory, that he may grant you a spirit of wisdom and revelation [of insight into mysteries and secrets] in the [deep and intimate] knowledge of Him.

Ephesians 1:18

I pray that the eyes of your heart be flooded with light, so that you can know and understand the hope to which He has called you, and how rich is His glorious inheritance in the saints (his set apart ones).

Colossians 1:10

That you may walk (live and conduct yourselves) in a manner worthy of the Lord, fully pleasing to him and desiring to please him in all things, bearing fruit in every good work and steadily growing and increasing in and by the knowledge of God [with fuller, deeper and clearer insight, acquaintance, and recognition].

Colossians 2:3

In Him all the treasures of [divine] wisdom (comprehensive insight into the ways and purposes of God) and [all the riches of spiritual] knowledge and enlightenment are stored up and lie hidden.

Colossians 3:16

Let the word [spoken by] Christ (the Messiah) have its home [in your hearts and minds] and dwell in you in [all its] richness, as you teach and admonish and train one another in all insight and intelligence and wisdom...

James 1:5

If any of you is deficient in wisdom, let him ask of the giving God [who gives] to everyone liberally and ungrudgingly, without reproaching or fault finding, and it will be given him.

18

Anti-Terror/Peace/ Freedom from Distress, Anxiety and Fear

Psalm 4:8

In peace I will both lie down and sleep, for you, Lord, alone make me dwell in safety and confident trust.

Psalm 9:9

The Lord will also be a refuge in a high tower for the oppressed, a refuge and a stronghold in times of trouble (high cost, destitution, and desperation).

Psalm 27:1

The Lord is my light and my salvation-whom shall I fear or dread? The Lord is the refuge and stronghold of my life - of whom shall I be afraid?

Psalm 34:4

I sought (inquired of) the Lord and required Him [of necessity and on the authority of His Word], and He heard me, and delivered me from all my fears.

Psalm 37:5

Commit your way to the Lord [roll and repose each care of your load on him]; trust (lean on, rely on, and be confident) also in him and he will bring it to pass.

Psalm 37:37

Mark the blameless man and behold the upright, for there is a happy and for the man of peace.

Psalm 46:1-3

God is our refuge and strength [mighty and impenetrable to temptation], a very present and well proved help in trouble. Therefore, we will not fear, though the earth should change and though the mountains be shaken into the midst of the Seas. Though its waters roar and foam, though the mountains tremble at its swelling and tumult. Selah [pause, and calmly think of that]!

Psalm 46:10

Let be and be still and know (recognize and understand) that I am God. I will be exalted among the nations! I will be exalted in the earth!

Psalm 56:3-4

What time I am afraid, I will have confidence in and put my trust and reliance in you. By [the help of] God I will praise his word; On God I lean, rely, and confidently put my trust; I will not fear. What can man, who is flesh, do to me?

Psalm 85:8

I will listen [with expectancy] to what God the Lord will say, for he will speak peace to his people, to his saints (those who are in right standing with him) - but let them not turn again to [self-confident] folly.

Psalm 91:5-6

You shall not be afraid of the terror of the night, nor of the arrow (the evil plots and slanders of the wicked) that flies by day, nor of the pestilence that stalks in darkness, nor of the destruction and sudden death that surprise and lay waste at noonday.

Psalm 94:12-13

Blessed (happy, fortunate, to be envied) is the man whom you discipline and instruct, O Lord, and teach out of your law, that you may give him power to keep himself calm in the days of adversity, until the [inevitable] pit of corruption is dug for the wicked.

Psalm 107:28-29

Then they cried to the Lord in their trouble, and he brings them out of their distresses. He hushes the storm to a calm and to a gentle whisper, so that the waves of the sea are still.

Psalm 118:6

The Lord is on my side; I will not fear. What can man do to me?

Psalm 119:165

Great peace have they who love your law; Nothing shall offend them or make them stumble.

Proverbs 3:2

For length of days and years of a life [worth living] and tranquility [inward and outward and continuing through old age till death], these shall they add to you.

Proverbs 14:30

A calm and undisturbed mind and heart are the life and health of the body...

Proverbs 16:7

When a man's ways please the Lord, he makes even his enemies to be at peace with him.

Isaiah 26:3

You will guard him and keep him in perfect and constant peace whose mind [both its inclination and its character] is stayed on you, because he commits himself to you, leans on you, and hopes confidently in you.

Isaiah 32:17

And the effect of righteousness will be peace [internal and external], and the result of righteousness will be quietness and confident trust forever.

Isaiah 41:10

Fear not [there is nothing to fear] for I am with you; Do not look around you in terror and be dismayed, for I am your God. I will strengthen and harden you to difficulties. Yes, I will help you; Yes, I will hold you up and retain you with my [victorious] right hand of rightness and justice.

Isaiah 54:10

For though the mountains should depart, and the hills be shaken or removed, yet My love and kindness shall not depart from you, nor shall My covenant of peace and completeness be removed, says the Lord, Who has compassion on you.

Isaiah 54:13

And all your children shall be disciples [taught by the Lord and obedient to His will], and great shall be the peace and undisturbed composure of your children.

Isaiah 54:7

But no weapon that is formed against you shall prosper, and every tongue that shall rise against you in judgment you shall show to be in the wrong. This [peace, righteousness, security, triumph over opposition] is the heritage of the servants of the Lord [those in whom the ideal servant of the Lord is reproduced]; this is the richest or the vindication which they obtained from me [this is that which I am part to them as their justification], says the Lord.

John 14:27

Peace I leave with you; My [own] peace I now give and bequeath to you. Not as the world gives do I give to you. Do not let your hearts be troubled, neither let them be afraid.

John 16:33

I have told you these things, so that in me you may have [perfect] peace and confidence. In the world you have tribulation and trials and distress and frustration but be of good cheer [take courage; be confident, certain, undaunted]! For

I have overcome the world. [I have deprived it of power to harm you and have conquered it for you.]

Philippians 4:6-7

Do not fret or have anxiety about anything, but in every circumstance in and in everything, by prayer and petition (definite requests), with Thanksgiving, continue to make your wants known to God. And God's peace shall be yours, that [tranquil state of a soul assured of its salvation through Christ, and so fearing nothing from God and being content with its earthly lot of whatever sort it that is, that peace] which transcends all understanding shall Garrison and mount guard over your hearts and minds in Christ Jesus.

Colossians 3:15

And let the peace (soul harmony which comes) from Christ rule (act as umpire continually) in your hearts [deciding and settling with finality all questions that arise in your minds, in that peaceful state] to which as [members of Christ's] one body you were also called [to live]. And be thankful (appreciative), [giving praise to God always].

Romans 8:31

And let the peace (soul harmony which comes) from Christ rule (act as umpire continually) in your hearts [deciding and settling with finality all questions that arise in your minds, in that peaceful state] to which as [members of Christ's] one body you were also called [to live]. And be thankful (appreciative), [giving praise to God always].

2 Timothy 1:7

For God did not give us a spirit of timidity (of cowardice, of craven and cringing and fawning fear), but [He has given us a spirit] of power and of love and of calm and well-balanced mind and discipline and self-control.

1 Peter 5:7

Casting the whole of your care [all your anxieties, all your worries, all your concerns, once and for all] on Him, for He cares for you affectionately and cares about you watchfully.

1 John 4:18

There is no fear in love [dread does not exist], but full-grown (complete, perfect) love turns fear out of doors and expels every trace of terror! For fear brings with it the thought of punishment, and [so] he who is afraid has not reached the full maturity of love [is not yet grown into love's complete perfection].

Ephesians 2:14

For He is [Himself] our peace (our bond of unity and harmony). He has made us both [Jew and Gentile] one [body], and has broken down (destroyed, abolished) the hostile dividing wall between us.

Ephesians 2:17

And He came and preached the glad tidings of peace to you who were afar off and [peace] to those who were near.

2 Timothy 2:22

Shun youthful lusts and flee from them and aim at and pursue righteousness (all that is virtuous and good, right living, conformity to the will of God in thought, word, and deed); [and aim at and pursue] faith, love, [and] peace (harmony and concord with others) in fellowship with all [Christians], who call upon the Lord out of a pure heart.

Hebrews 12:14

Strive to live in peace with everybody and pursue that consecration and holiness without which no one will [ever] see the Lord.

James 3:17

But the wisdom from above is first of all pure (undefiled); then it is peace loving, courteous (considerate, gentle). [It is willing to] yield to reason, full of compassion and good fruits; It is wholehearted and straightforward, impartial and unfeigned (free from doubts, wavering, and insincerity).

1 Peter 3:11

Let him turn away from wickedness and shun it and let him do right. Let him search for peace (harmony; undisturbedness from fears, agitating passions, and moral conflicts) and seek it eagerly. [Do not merely desire peaceful relations with God, with your fellow men, and with yourself, but pursue, go after them!]

19

JOY

Nehemiah 8:10

… be not grieved and depressed, for the joy of the Lord is your strength and stronghold.

Psalm 16:11

You will show me the path of life; In your presence is fullness of joy, at your right hand there are pleasures forevermore.

Psalm 30:5

For His anger is but for a moment, but His favor is for a lifetime or in His favor is life. Weeping may endure for a night, but joy comes in the morning.

Psalm 30:11

You have turned my mourning into dancing for me; You have put off my sackcloth and girded me with gladness.

Psalm 32:11

Be glad in the Lord and rejoice, you uncompromisingly righteous [you who are upright and in right standing with him]; shop for joy, all you upright and heart!

Psalm 33:21

For in Him does our heart rejoice, because we have trusted (relied on and been confident) in His holy name.

Psalm 42:5

Why are you cast down, O my inner self? And why should you moan over me and be disquieted within me? Hope in God and wait expectantly for him, for I shall yet praise him, my help and my God.

Psalm 51:12

Restore to me the joy of your salvation and uphold me with a willing spirit.

Psalm 92:4

For You, O Lord, have made me glad by Your works; at the deeds of Your hands I joyfully sing.

Psalm 126:1-3

When the Lord brought back the captives [who returned] to Zion, we were like those who dream [it seemed so unreal]. Then were our mouths filled with laughter, and our tongues was singing. Then they said among the nations, "the Lord has done great things for them." The Lord has done great things for us! We are glad!

Psalm 126:5

They who sow in tears shall reap in joy and singing.

Proverbs 15:15

All the days of desponding and afflicted are made evil [by anxious thoughts and forebodings], but he who has a glad heart has a continual feast [regardless of his circumstances].

Proverbs 15:23

A man has joy in making an apt answer, and a word spoken at the right moment-how good it is!

Proverbs 17:22

A happy heart is good medicine, and a cheerful (joyful) mind works healing...

Isaiah 12:3

Therefore with joy will you draw water from the wells of salvation.

Isaiah 61:1-3

...For the Lord has anointed me... to grant [consolation and joy] to those who mourn in Zion—to give them an ornament (a garland or diadem) of beauty instead of ashes, the oil of joy instead of mourning, the garment [expressive] of praise instead of a heavy, burdened, and failing spirit—that they may be called oaks of righteousness [lofty, strong, and magnificent, distinguished for uprightness, justice, and right standing with God], the planting of the Lord, that He may be glorified.

Isaiah 65:14

Behold, my servants shall sing for joy of heart...

Jeremiah 15:16

Your words were found, and I ate them; And your words were to me a joy and the rejoicing of my heart...

Jeremiah 31:13

Then will the maidens rejoice in the dance, and the young men and old together. For I will turn their mourning into joy and will comfort them and make them rejoice after their sorrow.

John 15:7, 11

If you live in me [abide vitally united to me] and my words remain in you and continue to live in your hearts, ask whatever you will, and it shall be done for you. I have told you these things, that my joy and delight may be in you, and that your joy and gladness may be a full measure and complete and overflowing.

Acts 3:19

So repent (change your mind and purpose); turn around and return [to God], that your sins may be erased (blotted out, wiped clean) that times of refreshing (of recovering from the effects of heat, of reviving with fresh air) may come from the presence of the Lord.

Romans 14:17

[After all] the kingdom of God is not a matter of [getting the] food and drink [one likes], but instead it is righteousness (that state which makes us a person acceptable to God) and [heart] peace and joy in the Holy Spirit.

Romans 15:13

May the God of your hope so fill you with all joy and peace in believing [through the experience of your faith] that by the power of the Holy Spirit you may abound and be overflowing (bubbling over) with hope.

Galatians 5:22

But the fruit of the [Holy] Spirit [the work which his presence within accomplishes] is love, joy (gladness), peace, patience (and even temper, forbearance) kindness, goodness (benevolence), faithfulness.

1 Peter 1:8

Without having seen Him, you love Him; though you do not [even] now see Him, you believe in Him and exult and thrill with inexpressible and glorious (triumphant, heavenly) joy.

Joy

20

SINGLES

Psalm 32:7

You are a hiding place for me; You, Lord, preserve me
from trouble, You surround me with songs and shouts of
deliverance. Selah [pause, and calmly think of that]!

Psalm 68:5-6

A father of the fatherless and a judge and protector of
the widows is God in his holy habitation. God places
the solitary in families and gives the desolate a home in
which to dwell; He leads the prisoners out to prosperity;
but the rebellious dwell in a parched land.

Proverbs 3:5-6

Lean on, trust in, and be confident in the Lord with all
your heart and mind and do not rely on your own insight
or understanding. In all your ways know, recognize, and
acknowledge him, and he will direct and make straight
and plain your paths.

Proverbs 18:22

He who finds a [true] wife finds a good thing and obtains
favor from the Lord.

Isaiah 34:16

Seek out the book of the Lord and read: not one of these [details of prophecy] shall fail, none shall want and lack her mate [in fulfillment]. For the mouth [of the Lord] has commanded, and his spirit has gathered them.

Isaiah 41:10-14

Fear not [there is nothing to fear], for I am with you; do not look around you in terror and be dismayed, for I am your God. I will strengthen and harden you to difficulties, yes, I will help you; yes, I will hold you up and retain you with My [victorious] right hand of rightness and justice. Behold, all they who are enraged and inflamed against you shall be put to shame and confounded; they who strive against you shall be as nothing and shall perish. You shall seek those who contend with you but shall not find them; they who war against you shall be as nothing, as nothing at all. For I the Lord your God hold your right hand; I am the Lord, who says to you, Fear not; I will help you! Fear not, you worm Jacob, you men of Israel! I will help you, says the Lord; your Redeemer is the Holy One of Israel.

Isaiah 45:2-3

I will go before you and level the mountains [to make the crooked places straight]; I will break in pieces the doors of bronze and cut asunder the bars of iron. And I will give you the treasures of darkness and hidden riches of secret places, that you may know that it is I, the Lord, the God of Israel, who calls you by your name.

Isaiah 54:4-10

Fear not, for you shall not be ashamed; neither be confounded and depressed, for you shall not be put to shame. For you shall forget the shame of your youth, and you shall not [seriously] remember the reproach of your widowhood any more. For your Maker is your Husband—the Lord of hosts is His name—and the Holy One of Israel is your Redeemer; the God of the whole earth He is called. For the Lord has called you like a woman forsaken, grieved in spirit, and heartsore—even a wife [wooed and won] in youth, when she is [later] refused and scorned, says your God. For a brief moment I forsook you, but with great compassion and mercy I will gather you [to Me] again. In a little burst of wrath I hid My face from you for a moment, but with age-enduring love and kindness I will have compassion and mercy on you, says the Lord, your Redeemer. For this is like the days of Noah to Me; as I swore that the waters of Noah should no more go over the earth, so have I sworn that I will not be angry with you or rebuke you. For though the mountains should depart and the hills be shaken or removed, yet My love and kindness shall not depart from you, nor shall My covenant of peace and completeness be removed, says the Lord, Who has compassion on you.

Isaiah 55:8-11

For My thoughts are not your thoughts, neither are your ways My ways, says the Lord. For as the heavens are higher than the earth, so are My ways higher than your ways and My thoughts than your thoughts. For as the rain and snow come down from the heavens, and return not there

Singles

again, but water the earth and make it bring forth and sprout, that it may give seed to the sower and bread to the eater, So shall My word be that goes forth out of My mouth: it shall not return to Me void [without producing any effect, useless], but it shall accomplish that which I please and purpose, and it shall prosper in the thing for which I sent it.

Isaiah 58:14

Then will you delight yourself in the Lord, and I will make you to ride on the high places of the earth, and I will feed you with the heritage [promised for you] of Jacob your father; for the mouth of the Lord has spoken it.

Jeremiah 29:11

For I know the thoughts and plans that I have for you, says the Lord, thoughts and plans for welfare and peace and not for evil, to give you hope in your final outcome.

Habakkuk 2:3

For the vision is yet for an appointed time and it hastens to the end [fulfillment]; it will not deceive or disappoint. Though it tarry, wait [earnestly] for it, because it will surely come; It will not be behindhand on its appointed day.

Matthew 6:20-24

But gather and heap up and store for yourselves treasures in heaven, where neither moth nor rust nor worm consume and destroy, and where thieves do not break through and steal; For where your treasure is, there will your heart be also. The eye is the lamp of the body. So, if your eye is sound, your entire body will be full of light.

But if your eye is unsound, your whole body will be full of darkness. If then the very light in you [your conscience] is darkened, how dense is that darkness! No one can serve two masters; for either he will hate the one and love the other, or he will stand by and be devoted to the one and despise and be against the other. You cannot serve God and mammon (deceitful riches, money, possessions, or whatever is trusted in).

Colossians 2:10

And you are in him, made full and having come to fullness of life [in Christ you to are filled with the godhead-father, son and Holy Spirit-and reach full spiritual stature]. and he is the head of all rule and authority [of every angelic principality and power].

Singles

21

OVERCOMING WEIGHT, BONDAGES AND OTHER HABITS

Psalm 18:29

For by you I can run through a troop, and by my God I can leap over a wall.

Psalm 37:4

Delight yourself also in the Lord, and he will give you the desires and secret petitions of your heart.

Proverbs 23:1-3

When you sit down to eat with a ruler, consider who and what are before you; For you will put a knife to your throat if you are a man given to desire. Be not desirous of his dainties, for it is deceitful food [offered with questionable motives].

Proverbs 25:16

Have you found [pleasure sweet like] honey? Eat only as much as is sufficient for you, less being filled with it, you vomit it.

Matthew 10:1

And Jesus summoned to him his twelve disciples and gave them power and authority over unclean spirits, to drive them out, and to cure all kinds of disease and all kinds of weakness and infirmity.

Luke 21:34

But take heed to yourselves and be on your guard, lest your hearts be overburdened and depressed (weighted down) with the giddiness and headache and nausea of self-indulgence, drunkenness, and worldly worries and cares pertaining to [the business of] this life, and [lest] that day come upon you suddenly like a trap or a noose.

John 8:32

And you will know the truth, and the truth will set you free.

John 8:36

So, if the Son liberates you [makes you free men], then you are really and unquestionably free.

John 10:10

The thief comes only in order to steal and kill and destroy. I came that they may have and enjoy life, and have it in abundance (to the full, till it overflows).

Acts 10:38

How God anointed and consecrated Jesus of Nazareth with the [Holy] Spirit and with strength and ability and power; how He went about doing good and, in particular, curing all who were harassed and oppressed by [the power of] the devil, for God was with Him.

Acts 16:18

And she did this for many days. Then Paul, being sorely annoyed and worn out, turned and said to the spirit within her, "I charge you in the name of Jesus Christ to come out of her!" And it came out that very moment.

Acts 24:16

Therefore, I always exercise and discipline myself [mortifying my body, deadening my carnal affections, bodily appetites, and worldly desires, endeavoring in all respects] to have a clear (unshaken, blameless) conscience, void of offense toward God and toward men.

Romans 6:12-14

Let not sin therefore rule as king in your mortal (short-lived, perishable) bodies, to make you yield to its cravings and be subject to its lusts and evil passions. Do not continue offering or yielding your bodily members [and faculties] to sin as instruments (tools) of wickedness. But offer and yield yourselves to God as though you have been raised from the dead to [perpetual] life, and your bodily members [and faculties] to God, presenting them as implements of righteousness. For sin shall not [any longer] exert dominion over you.

Romans 6:18,22

And having been set free from sin, you have become the servants of righteousness (of conformity to the divine will in thought, purpose, and action). But now since you have been set free from sin and have become the slaves of God, you have your present reward in holiness and its end is eternal life.

Romans 8:1

Therefore, [there is] now no condemnation (no adjudging guilty of wrong) for those who are in Christ Jesus, who live [and] walk not after the dictates of the flesh, but after the dictates of the Spirit.

Romans 8:3

For God has done what the law could not do, [its power] being weakened by the flesh [the entire nature of man without the Holy Spirit]. Sending His own Son in the guise of sinful flesh and as an offering for sin, [God] condemned sin in the flesh [subdued, overcame, deprived it of its power over all who accept that sacrifice].

Romans 8:12-13

So then, brethren, we are debtors, but not to the flesh [we are not obligated to our carnal nature], to live [a life ruled by the standards set up by the dictates] of the flesh. For if you live according to [the dictates of] the flesh, you will surely die. But if through the power of the [Holy] Spirit you are [habitually] putting to death (making extinct, deadening) the [evil] deeds prompted by the body, you shall [really and genuinely] live forever.

Romans 8:37

Yet amid all these things we are more than conquerors and gain a surpassing victory through Him Who loved us.

1 Corinthians 6:12

Everything is permissible (allowable and lawful) for me; but not all things are helpful (good for me to do, expedient and profitable when considered with other things). Everything is lawful for me, but I will not become the slave of anything or be brought under its power.

1 Corinthians 9:27

But [like a boxer] I buffet my body [handle it roughly, discipline it by hardships] and subdue it, for fear that after proclaiming to others the gospel and things pertaining to it, I myself should become unfit [not stand the test, be unapproved and rejected as a counterfeit].

1 Corinthians 10:13-14

For no temptation (no trial regarded as enticing to sin), [no matter how it comes or where it leads] has overtaken you and laid hold on you that is not common to man [that is, no temptation or trial has come to you that is beyond human resistance and that is not adjusted and adapted and belonging to human experience, and such as man can bear]. But God is faithful [to His Word and to His compassionate nature], and He [can be trusted] not to let you be tempted and tried and assayed beyond your ability and strength of resistance and power to endure, but with the temptation He will [always] also provide the way out (the means of escape to a landing place), that you may be capable and strong and powerful to bear up under it patiently. Therefore, my dearly beloved, shun (keep clear away from, avoid by flight if need be) any sort of idolatry (of loving or venerating anything more than God).

2 Corinthians 2:14

But thanks be to God, Who in Christ always leads us in triumph [as trophies of crossed victory] and through US spreads it makes evident the fragrance of the knowledge of God everywhere.

2 Corinthians 3:5

Not that we are fit (qualified and sufficient inability) of ourselves to form personal judgments or to claim or to count anything as coming from us, but our power and ability and sufficiency are from God.

2 Corinthians 5:17

Therefore, if any person is [ingrafted] in Christ (the Messiah) he is a new creation (a new creature altogether); the old [previous mortal and spiritual condition] has passed away. Behold the fresh and new has come!

2 Corinthians 7:1

Therefore, since these [great] promises are ours, beloved, let us cleanse ourselves from everything that contaminates and defiles our body and spirit, and bring [hour consecration to completeness in the [reverential] fear of God.

2 Corinthians 12:9-10

But He said to me, My grace (My favor and loving-kindness and mercy) is enough for you [sufficient against any danger and enables you to bear the trouble manfully]; for My strength and power are made perfect (fulfilled and completed) and show themselves most effective in [your] weakness. Therefore, I will all the more gladly glory in my weaknesses and infirmities, that the strength and power of Christ (the Messiah) may rest (yes, may pitch a tent over and dwell) upon me! So for the sake of Christ, I am well pleased and take pleasure in infirmities, insults, hardships, persecutions, perplexities and distresses; for when I am weak [in human strength], then am I [truly] strong (able, powerful in divine strength).

Galatians 5:1

In [this] freedom Christ has made us free [and completely liberated us]; stand fast then, and do not be hampered and held ensnared and submit again to a yoke of slavery [which you have once put off].

2 Timothy 1:7

For God did not give us a spirit of timidity (of cowardice, of craven and cringing and fawning fear), but [he has given us a spirit] of power and of love and of a calm and well-balanced mind and discipline and self-control.

James 4:7

So be subject to God. Resist the devil [stand firm against him], and he will flee from you.

1 Peter 4:12

Beloved, do not be amazed and bewildered at the fiery ordeal which is taking place to test your quality, as though something strange (unusual and alien to you and your position) were befalling you.

2 Peter 2:19

They promise them liberty, when they themselves are slaves of depravity and defilement-for by whatever anyone is made inferior or worse or is overcome, to that [person or thing] he is enslaved.

1 John 4:4

Little children, you are of God [you belong to Him] and have [already] defeated and overcome them [the agents of the antichrist], because He Who lives in you is greater (mightier) than he who is in the world.

1 John 5:21

Little children, keep yourselves from idols (false gods) — [from anything and everything that would occupy the place in your heart due to God, from any sort of substitute for Him that would take first place in your life]. Amen (so let it be).

22

Employment

Psalm 1:3

And he shall be like a tree firmly planted [and tended] by the streams of water, ready to bring forth its fruit in its season; its leaf also shall not fade or wither; and everything he does shall prosper [and come to maturity].

Psalm 128:2

For you shall eat [the fruit] of the labor of your hands; happy (blessed, fortunate, enviable) shall you be, and it shall be well with you.

Proverbs 10:4

He becomes poor who works with the slack and idle hand, but the hand of the diligent makes rich.

Proverbs 21:5

The thoughts of the [steadily] diligent tend only to plenteous isness, but everyone who is impatient and hasty hastens only to want.

Proverbs 28:19

He who cultivates his land will have plenty of bread, but he who follows worthless people and pursuits will have poverty enough.

Isaiah 48:17

Thus says the Lord, your Redeemer, the holy one of Israel: I am the Lord your God, who teaches you to profit, who leads you in the way that you should go.

Romans 4:4

Now to a laborer, his wages are not counted as a favor or a gift, but as an obligation (something owed to him).

1 Thessalonians 4:12

So that you may bear yourselves becomingly and be correct and honorable and command the respect of the outside world, being dependent on nobody [self-supporting] and having need of nothing.

Titus 3:14

And let our own [people really] learn to apply themselves to good deeds (to honest labor and honorable employment), so that they may be able to meet necessary demands whenever the occasion may require and not be living idle and uncultivated and unfruitful lives.

Revelation 3:8

I know your [record] of works and what you are doing. See! I have set before you a door wide open which no one is able to shut; I know that you have but little power, and yet you have kept my word and guarded my message and have not renounced or denied my name.

23

Prayer for Receiving

Psalm 37:2-4

Fret not yourself... trust (lean on, rely on, and be confident) in the Lord... delight yourself also in the Lord, and he will give you the desires and secret petitions of your heart.

Proverbs 10:22

The blessing of the Lord - it makes [truly] rich, and he adds no sorrow with it [neither does toiling increase it].

Proverbs 10:24

The thing a wicked man fears shall come upon him, but the desire of the uncompromisingly righteous shall be granted.

Matthew 18:19

Again, I tell you, if two of you on earth agree (harmonize together, make a symphony together) about whatever [anything and everything] they may ask, it will come to pass and be done for them by my father in heaven.

Matthew 21:21-22

And Jesus answered them, "Truly I say to you, if you have faith (a firm relying trust) and do not doubt, you will not only do what has been done to the victory, but even if you say to this mountain, 'be taken up and cast into the sea,' it will be done. And whatever you ask for in prayer, having faith and [really] believing, you will receive."

Mark 11:24

Truly I tell you, who never says to this mountain, "Be lifted up and thrown into the sea!" And does not doubt at all in his heart but believes that what he says will take place it will be done for him. For this reason, I am telling you, whatever you ask for in prayer, believe (trust and be confident) that it is granted to you, and you will [get it].

John 14:13

And I will do [I myself will grant] whatever you ask in my name [as presenting all that I am], so that the father may be glorified and extolled in (through) the Son.

John 15:7

If you live in me [abide vitally united to me] and my words remain in you and continue to live in your hearts, ask whatever you will, and it shall be done for you.

John 16:23

And when that time comes, you will ask nothing of me [you will need to ask me no questions]. I assure you, most solemnly I tell you, that my father will grant you whatever you ask in my name [as presenting all that I AM].

Philippians 4:6

Do not fret or have any anxiety about anything, but in every circumstance and in everything, by prayer and petition (definite requests), with thanksgiving, continue to make your wants known to God.

1 John 5:14-15

And this is the confidence (the assurance, the privilege of boldness) which we have in him: [we are sure] that if we ask anything (make any request) according to his will (in agreement with his own plan), he listens to and hears us. And if (since) we [positively] know that he listens to us in whatever we ask, we also know [with settled and absolute knowledge] that we have [granted us as our present possessions] the request made of him.

Receiving

24

FAVOR

Psalm 5:12

For you shall eat [the fruit] of the labor of your hands; happy (blessed, fortunate, enviable) shall you be, and it shall be well with you.

Psalm 30:5

For His anger is but for a moment, but His favor is for a lifetime or in His favor is life…

Psalm 41:11

By this I know that you favor and delight in me, because my enemy does not triumph over me.

Psalm 90:17

And let the beauty and delightfulness in favor of our Lord our God be upon us; Confirm and establish the work of our hands yes, the work of our hands, confirm and establish it.

Psalm 112:5

It is well with the man who deals generously and lends, who conducts his affairs with justice.

Proverbs 3:1-4

Forget not my law...for length of days and years of a life [worth living] and tranquility [inward and outward and continuing through old age till death], these shall they add to you. Let not mercy and kindness [shutting out all hatred and selfishness] and truth [shutting out all deliberate hypocrisy or falsehood] forsake you; bind them about your neck, write them upon the tablet of your heart. So shall you find favor, good understanding, and high esteem in the sight [or judgment] of God and man.

Proverbs 8:35

For whoever finds me [wisdom] finds life and draws forth and obtains favor from the Lord.

Proverbs 11:27

He who diligently seeks good seeks [God's] favor, but he who searches after evil, it shall come upon him.

Proverbs 12:24

The hand of the diligent will rule, but the slothful will be put to forced labor.

Proverbs 13:15

Good understanding wins favor, but the way of the transgressor is hard [like the barren, dry soil or the impassable swamp].

Proverbs 16:17

When a man's ways please the Lord, He makes even his enemies to be at peace with him.

Proverbs 18:22

He who finds a [true] wife finds a good thing and obtains favor from the Lord.

Luke 1:30

And the angel said to her, "Do not be afraid, Mary, for you have found grace (free, spontaneous, absolute favor and loving kindness) with God."

Acts 7:10

And delivered him from all his distressing afflictions and won him goodwill and favor and wisdom and understanding in the sight of Pharaoh...

Romans 5:20

...But where sin increased and abounded, grace (God's unmerited favor) has surpassed it and increased the more and the superabounded.

2 Corinthians 8:9

For you are becoming progressively acquainted with and recognizing more strongly and clearly the grace of our Lord Jesus Christ (His kindness, His gracious generosity, His undeserved favor and spiritual blessing), [in] that though He was [so very] rich, yet for your sakes He became [so very] poor, in order that by His poverty you might become enriched (abundantly supplied).

Favor

25

SPEECH

Job 22:28

You shall also decide and decree a thing, and it shall be established for you; And the light [of God's favor] shall shine upon your ways.

Psalm 145:11

They shall speak of the glory of your Kingdom and talk of your power.

Proverbs 4:23-24

Keep and guard your heart with all vigilance and above all that you guard, for out of it flow the springs of life. Put away from you false and dishonest speech, and willful and contrary talk put it far from you.

Proverbs 5:2

That you may exercise proper discrimination and discretion and your lips may guard and keep knowledge and the wise answer [to temptation.]

Proverbs 6:2

You are snared with the words of your lips, you are caught by the speech of your mouth.

Proverbs 8:6-8

Hear, for I will speak excellent in princely things; And the opening of my lips shall be for right things. For my mouth shall utter truth, and wrongdoing is detestable and loathsome to my lips. All the words of my mouth are righteous (upright and in right standing with God); there is nothing contrary to truth or crooked in them.

Proverbs 10:11

The mouth of the uncompromisingly righteous man is a well of life…

Proverbs 10:20

The tongues of those who are upright and in right standing with God are as choice silver…

Proverbs 10:21

The lips of the uncompromisingly righteous feet and God many…

Proverbs 10:31

The mouths of the righteous (those harmonious with God) bring forth skillful and godly wisdom…

Proverbs 10:32

The lips of the uncompromisingly righteous know [and therefore utter] what is acceptable, but the mouth of the wicked knows [and therefore speaks only] what is obstinately willful and contrary.

Proverbs 11:13

He who goes about as a tail bearer reveals secrets, but he who is trustworthy and faithful in spirit keeps the matter hidden.

Proverbs 12:14

From the fruit of his words a man shall be satisfied with good, and the work of a man's hands shall come back to him [as a harvest].

Proverbs 12:18

...the tongue of the wise brings healing.

Proverbs 12:19

Truthful lips shall be established forever...

Proverbs 12:25

...and encouraging word makes the heart glad.

Proverbs 13:2

A good man eats good from the fruit of his mouth...

Proverbs 13:3

He who guards his mouth keeps his life, but he who opens wide his lips comes to ruin.

Proverbs 14:3

...the wise men's lips preserve him.

Proverbs 14:14

...a good man shall be satisfied with [the fruit of] his ways [with the holy thoughts and actions which his heart prompts and in which he delights].

Proverbs15:1-2

A soft answer turns away wrath... the tongue of the wise utters knowledge rightly...

Proverbs 15:4

A gentle tongue [with its healing power] is a tree of life...

Proverbs 15:23

A man has joy in making an appt answer, and a word spoken at the right moment- how good it is!

Proverbs 15:26

...the words of the pure are pleasing words to Him.

Proverbs 16:13

Right and just lips are the delight of a king...

Proverbs 16:21

... winsome speech increases learning [in both speaker and listener].

Proverbs 16:23-24

The mind of the wise instructs his mouth, and adds learning and persuasiveness to his lips, pleasant words are as a honeycomb, sweet to the mind and healing to the body.

Proverbs 17:9

He who covers and forgives an offense seeks love, but he who repeats or harps on a matter separates even close friends.

Proverbs 17:14

The beginning of strife is when water first trickles [from a crack in a dam]; therefore, stop contention before it becomes worse, and quarreling breaks out.

Proverbs 17:20

…He who has a willful and contrary tongue will fall into calamity.

Proverbs 17:27

He who has knowledge spares his words…

Proverbs 17:28

Even a fool when he holds his peace is considered wise; When he closes his lips, he is esteemed a man of understanding.

Proverbs 18:4

The words of a [discreet and wise] man's mouth are like deep waters [plenteous and difficult to fathom], and the fountain of skillful and godly wisdom is like a gushing stream [sparkling, fresh, pure, and life giving].

Proverbs 18:6-8

A [self-confident] fools lips bring contention, and his mouth invites a beating. A [self-confident] fool's mouth is his ruin, and his lips are a snare to himself. The words of a whisper or tail bearer are as dainty morsels; They go down into the innermost parts of the body.

Proverbs18:20-21

A man's [moral] self shall be filled with the fruit of his mouth; And with the consequence of his words he must be satisfied [whether good or evil]. Death and life are in the power of the tongue, and they who indulge in it shall eat the fruit of it [for death or life].

Proverbs 20:19

He who goes about as a tail bearer reveals secret; Therefore associate not with him who talks too freely.

Proverbs 21:23

He who guards his mouth and his tongue keeps himself from troubles.

Proverbs 21:28

A false witness will perish, but the word of a man who hears attentively will endure and go unchallenged.

Proverbs 25:11

A word fitly spoken in due season is like apples of gold in settings of silver.

Proverbs 26:20

For the lack of wood the fire goes out, and where there is no whisperer, contingency cases.

Proverbs 26:22

The words of a whisperer or slander are like dainty morsels or words of sport [to some, but to others are like deadly wounds]; and they go down into the innermost parts of the body [or the victim's nature].

Proverbs 26:28

A lying tongue hates those it wounds and crushes, and a flattering mouth works ruin.

Proverbs 27:2

Let another man praise you, and not your own mouth; A stranger, and not your own lips.

Proverbs 29:11

A [self-confident] fool utters all his anger, but a wise man holds it back and stills it.

Proverbs 31:8-9

Open your mouth for the dumb [those unable to speak for themselves], for the rights of all who are left desolate and defenseless. Open your mouth, judge righteously, and administer justice for the poor and needy.

Proverbs 31:26

She opens her mouth in skillful and godly wisdom, and on her tongue is the law of kindness [giving counsel and instruction].

Isaiah 50:4

The servant of God says, "the Lord God has given me the tongue of a disciple and of one who is taught, that I should know how to speak a word in season to him who is weary. He wakens me morning by morning; he wakens my ear to hear as a disciple [as one who is taught]."

Isaiah 55:11

So shall my word be that goes forth out of my mouth: it shall not return to me void [without producing any effect, useless], but it shall accomplish that which I please and purpose, and it shall prosper in the thing for which I sent it.

Isaiah 59:21

As for me, this is my covenant or league with them, says the Lord: my spirit, who is upon you [and who writes the law of God inwardly on the heart], and my words which I have put in your mouth shall not depart out of your mouth, or out of the mouths of your [true spiritual] children, or out of the mouths of your children's children, says the Lord, from henceforth and forever.

Matthew 8:8

But the centurion replied to him, "Lord, I am not worthy or fit to have you come under my roof; But only speak the word, and my servant boy will be cured."

Matthew 12:34-35

...for out of the fullness (the overflow, the superabundance) of the heart the mouth speaks. The good man from his inner good treasure flings forth good things, and the evil man out of his inner evil storehouse flings forth evil things.

Matthew 15:11

It is not what goes into the mouth of a man that makes him unclean and defiled, but what comes out of the mouth; This makes a man unclean and defiles [him].

Colossians 4:6

Let your speech at all times be gracious (pleasant and winsome), seasoned [as it were] with salt, [so that you may never be at a loss] to know how you ought to answer anyone [who puts a question to you].

James 3:6

And the tongue is a fire. The tongue is a world of wickedness set among our members, contaminating and depraving the whole body and setting on fire the wheel of birth (the cycle of man's nature) ...

26

~~~

Waiting on God

Psalm 25:4-5

Show me your ways, O Lord; Teach me your paths. Guide me in your truth and faithfulness and teach me, for you are the God of my salvation; for you [you only an altogether] do I wait [expectantly] all the day long.

Psalm 27:14

Wait and hope for and expect the Lord; Be brave and of good courage and let your heart be stout and enduring. Yes, wait for and hope for and expect the Lord.

Psalm 31:24

Be strong and let your heart take courage, all you who wait for and hope for and expect the Lord!

Psalm 33:18-22

Behold, the Lord's eye is upon those who fear him [who revere and worship him with awe], who wait for him and hope in his mercy and loving kindness, to deliver them from death and keep them alive and famine. Our inner selves wait [earnestly] for the Lord; He is our help and our shield. For in him does our heart rejoice, because we have trusted (relied on and been confident) in his holy name. Let your mercy and loving kindness, O Lord, be upon us, in proportion to our waiting and hoping for you.

Psalm 37:7-9, 34

Be still and rest in the Lord; wait for Him and patiently lean yourself upon Him; fret not yourself because of him who prospers in his way, because of the man who brings wicked devices to pass. Cease from anger and forsake wrath; fret not yourself—it tends only to evildoing. For evildoers shall be cut off, but those who wait and hope and look for the Lord [in the end] shall inherit the earth. Wait for and expect the Lord and keep and heed His way, and He will exalt you to inherit the land; [in the end] when the wicked are cut off, you shall see it.

Psalm 40:3

And He has put a new song in my mouth, a song of praise to our God. Many shall see and fear (revere and worship) and put their trust and confident reliance in the Lord.

Psalm 62:1

For God alone my soul waits in silence; From him comes my salvation.

Psalm 63:1-2

O God, You are my God, earnestly will I seek you; My inner self thirst for you, my flesh longs and is faint for you, in a dry and weary land where no water is. So, I have looked upon you in the sanctuary to see your power and your glory.

Psalm 69:6

Let not those who wait and hope and look for you, O Lord of host, be put to shame through me; Let not those who seek and inquire for and require you [as their vital necessity] be brought to confusion and dishonor through me, O God of Israel.

Psalm 104:27-29

These all wait and are dependent upon you, that you may give them their food and due season. When you give it to them, they gather it up; You open your hand, and they are filled with good things. When you hide your face, they are troubled and dismayed; When you take away their breath they die and return to their dust.

Psalm 106:13

But they hastily forget his works; They did not [earnestly] wait for his plans [to develop] regarding them.

Psalm 130:5-6

I wait for the Lord, I expectantly wait, and in his word do, I hope. I am looking and waiting for the Lord more than watchmen for the morning, I say more than watchmen for the morning.

Psalm 145:14-15

The Lord upholds all those [of His own] who are falling and raises up all those who are bowed down. The eyes of all wait for You [looking, watching, and expecting] and You give them their food in due season.

Isaiah 26:8-9

Yes, in the path of Your judgments, O Lord, we wait [expectantly] for You; our heartfelt desire is for Your name and for the remembrance of You. My soul yearns for You [O Lord] in the night, yes, my spirit within me seeks You earnestly; for [only] when Your judgments are in the earth will the inhabitants of the world learn righteousness (uprightness and right standing with God).

Isaiah 30:15, 18

For thus said the Lord God, the Holy One of Israel: In returning [to Me] and resting [in Me] you shall be saved; in quietness and in [trusting] confidence shall be your strength. But you would not. And therefore, the Lord [earnestly] waits [expecting, looking, and longing] to be gracious to you; and therefore, He lifts Himself up, that He may have mercy on you and show loving-kindness to you. For the Lord is a God of justice. Blessed (happy, fortunate, to be envied) are all those who [earnestly] wait for Him, who expect and look and long for Him [for His victory, His favor, His love, His peace, His joy, and His matchless, unbroken companionship]!

Isaiah 40:30-31

Even youths shall faint and be weary, and [selected] young men shall feebly stumble and fall exhausted; But those who wait for the Lord [who expect, look for, and hope in Him] shall change and renew their strength and power; they shall lift their wings and mount up [close to God] as eagles [mount up to the sun]; they shall run and not be weary, they shall walk and not faint or become tired.

Isaiah 64:4

For from of old no one has heard nor perceived by the ear, nor has the eye seen a God besides You, who works and shows Himself active on behalf of him who [earnestly] waits for Him.

Jeremiah 29:13

Then you will seek Me, inquire for, and require Me [as a vital necessity] and find Me when you search for Me with all your heart.

Lamentations 3:25

The Lord is good to those who wait hopefully and expectantly for Him, to those who seek Him [inquire of and for Him and require him by right of necessity and on the authority of God's Word].

Luke 11:19

So, I say to you, "ask and keep on asking and it shall be given you; seek and keep on seeking and you shall find; knock and keep on knocking and the door shall be opened to you."

Luke 24:49

And behold, I will send forth upon you what My Father has promised; But remain in the city [Jerusalem] until you are clothed with power from on high.

John 12:32

And I, if and when I am lifted up from the earth [on the cross], we'll draw and attract all men [Gentiles as well as Jews] to Myself.

Acts 1:4-8

And while being in their company and eating with them, He commanded them not to leave Jerusalem but to wait for what the Father had promised, of which [He said] you have heard Me speak. For John baptized with water, but not many days from now you shall be baptized with (placed in, introduced into) the Holy Spirit. So, when they were assembled, they asked Him, Lord, is this the time when You will reestablish the kingdom and restore it to Israel? He said to them, it is not for you to become acquainted with and know what time brings [the things and events of time and their definite periods] or fixed years and seasons (their critical niche in time), which the Father has appointed (fixed and reserved) by His own choice and authority and personal power. But you shall receive power (ability, efficiency, and might) when the Holy Spirit has come upon you, and you shall be My witnesses in Jerusalem and all Judea and Samaria and to the ends (the very bounds) of the earth.

2 Corinthians 3:17

Now the Lord is the spirit, and where the spirit of the Lord is, there is liberty (emancipation from bondage, freedom).

1 Timothy 4:8

For physical training is of some value (useful for a little), but godliness (spiritual training) is useful and a value in everything and in every way, for it holds the promise for the present life and also for the life which is to come.

Hebrews 10:36

For you have need of steadfast patience and endurance, so that you may perform and fully accomplish the will of God, and thus receive and carry away [and enjoy to the full] what is promised.

James 1:4

But let endurance and steadfastness and patience have full play and do a thorough work, so that you may be [people] perfectly and fully developed [with no defects], lacking in nothing.

Waiting on God

Please visit our website arboministries.org
for more information on how to purchase
other books and audio messages.

If you would like to have Steve and Barbara
minister in your area,
please contact our office at
1-800-276-2726.

Additional contact information:

Arbo Ministries
14 Curtis Road
Gilford, New Hampshire 03249

arboministries@gmail.com

You can also follow our ministry
on Facebook at New England Sanctuary
or on YouTube @barbarastevearbo.

Ingram Content Group UK Ltd.
Milton Keynes UK
UKHW050619240723
425659UK00010B/56